1 & 2 THESSALONIANS

A Bible Commentary in the Wesleyan Tradition

WARREN WOOLSEY

General Publisher: Nathan Birky
General Editor: Ray E. Barnwell
Managing Editor: Russell Gunsalus
Senior Editor: David Higle
Editor: Kelly Trennepohl
Editorial Assistant: Gail Whitmire

CONTENTS

EDITOR'S PREFACE

This book is part of a series of commentaries seeking to interpret the books of the Bible from a Wesleyan perspective. It is designed primarily for lay people, especially teachers of Sunday school and leaders of Bible studies. Pastors will also find this series very helpful. In addition, this series is also for people who want to read and study on their own for spiritual edification.

Each book of the Bible will be explained paragraph by paragraph. This "wide-angle lens" approach helps the reader to follow the primary flow of thought in each passage. This, in turn, will help the reader to avoid "missing the forest because of the trees," a problem many people encounter when reading commentaries.

At the same time, the authors slow down often to examine particular details and concepts that are important for understanding the bigger picture. Where there are alternative understandings of key passages, the authors acknowledge these so the reader will experience a broader knowledge of the various theological traditions and how the Wesleyan perspective relates to them.

These commentaries follow the New International Version and are intended to be read with your Bible open. With this in mind, the biblical text is not reproduced in full, but appears in bold type throughout the discussion of each passage. Greater insight will be gained by reading along in your Bible as you read the commentaries.

These volumes do not replace the valuable technical commentaries that offer in-depth grammatical and textual analysis. What they do offer is an interpretation of the Bible that we hope will lead to a greater understanding of what the Bible says, its significance for our lives today, and further transformation into the image of Christ.

David A. Higle
Senior Editor

AUTHOR'S PREFACE

In the preface to his *Explanatory Notes upon the New Testament*, John Wesley described the readers he hoped primarily to serve: not "men of learning, who are provided with many other helps," but rather those "who understand only their mother tongue, and yet reverence and love the word of God, and have a desire to save their souls."[1] This author does not pretend to the classical learning of Oxford-educated John Wesley, M.A., but he does share in Wesley's declared purpose.

This commentary is intended to facilitate the interpretation and application of the Apostle Paul's letters to the Thessalonians by men and women like John Wesley's intended readers: (1) they *revere* the Scriptures; they acknowledge them to be the word of God, which is "living and active," and which "penetrates" and "judges the thoughts and attitudes of the heart" (Hebrews 4:12); (2) they *love* the Scriptures; they say with the psalmist, "Your statutes . . . are the joy of my heart. My heart is set on keeping your decrees to the very end" (Psalm 119:111-112); and (3) They "desire to save their souls"; they *submit* to the Scriptures; they read with the intention to obey. They are ready to be taught, rebuked, corrected, trained in righteousness, so as to be "thoroughly equipped for every good work" (2 Timothy 3:16-17); they aspire to that obedience which is true freedom (see Psalm 119:44-45; James 1:25).

I must put on record my appreciation to the Department of Local Church Education of The Wesleyan Church for this invitation to immerse myself in Paul's Thessalonian letters. Special thanks are due the Rev. David Higle without whose editorial guidance this work would be marked by even more deficiencies. Other staff members have made significant contributions. Most of all, I am grateful to my wife, Ella, for patience and understanding when this project required that other items, rightly on the agenda, be deferred.

ENDNOTE

[1]John Wesley, "Explanatory Notes upon the New Testament," in *The Works of John Wesley,* vol. 14 (Grand Rapids, Michigan: Zondervan Publishing House, n.d.), p. 235.

INTRODUCTION

Tucked away behind the Apostle Paul's major letters in the New Testament are two letters which breathe the new life imparted to the church by the risen Christ in the exciting early days of the Christian era. These Thessalonian letters also reveal the beating heart and incisive intellect of the Apostle Paul, probably the most effective church planter in all of Christian history.

First Thessalonians has most often been used from the pulpit for teaching on the second coming of Christ or on sanctification, but these letters also have much to teach us about the life and work of God's church. As relatively new Christians, the Thessalonians had much to learn, but even at that stage, Paul described them as a "model" church (1 Thess. 1:7). They were an example for other Christians then, and although our circumstances now are very different, we may be confident that these letters have been included in Holy Scripture for the benefit of later generations of Christians, including ourselves. As Paul wrote the Corinthians concerning the Old Testament, "these things happened to them as examples and were written down as warnings for us, on whom the fulfillment of the ages has come" (1 Cor. 10:11).

More clearly in 1 Thessalonians than in any other single letter, we have presented to us the picture of Paul as model pastor. He was ready, simultaneously or by turns, to be to his spiritual children a father (1 Thess. 2:11), mother (2:7), and brother (1:4 and throughout the letter). When he was among them, he poured his life into the church by preaching and teaching, while also laboring night and day so as not to be a burden to them (2:9). When painfully separated from them (2:17) and, for a time, anxious (3:5), he toiled for them in prayer with both concern and confidence (1:2-5; 3:10-13). And he continued to minister to them pastorally in the only way he could at the moment: by writing this letter crammed with reminders, instructions, warnings, and encouragement.

The early church accorded 2 Thessalonians its position immediately *after* 1 Thessalonians among the letters of the New Testament, not because it is the shorter of the two (though that may have been a factor in their thinking), but because they believed it to be second *historically*.

That is, they viewed it as a follow-up letter by Paul to essentially the same congregation as 1 Thessalonians, a letter made necessary by several ongoing problems in the life of the church.

This appraisal of both authorship and relation to 1 Thessalonians has been challenged by a number of New Testament scholars over the last century, especially in recent decades. A typical position statement excludes it from a place among the *"unquestionably* authentic Pauline letters," while acknowledging that it is regarded as Pauline by "probably the majority of interpreters."[1]

The issues raised are complex, and frequently the discussion is very technical. To evaluate many of the arguments proposed requires expert knowledge of the Greek language and intimate acquaintance with the Mediterranean world of the first century. That level of critical evaluation lies beyond the scope and purpose of this commentary. (For a brief and accessible overview of the issues, see Leon Morris[2]; for a more thorough treatment, see I. Howard Marshall.[3])

This commentary proceeds on the basis of the time-tested view of 2 Thessalonians, which is also the opinion of the majority of New Testament scholars, many of them not precommitted to conservative conclusions. I understand it to be written by the Apostle Paul (with his colleagues) to the same congregation in Thessalonica addressed in 1 Thessalonians, probably only a short time later.

AUTHORSHIP

Scholarly opinion is virtually unanimous in attributing 1 Thessalonians to the Apostle Paul. Although it is probably the earliest among his letters which have been preserved for us (some respected scholars think that the Epistle to the Galatians was written earlier), Paul was near the height of his apostolic career; already he was an experienced cross-cultural missionary.

Immediately following his conversion, Paul preached in and around Damascus for nearly three years (see Acts 9:20-25; Galatians 1:17-18), and then in Syria and Cilicia for some eight or ten years (Gal. 1:21-24; see Acts 15:41, which mentions churches he must have planted then).[4] After at least a year on the ministry team at Antioch (Acts 11:25-26; 13:1), his "first missionary journey" took him and Barnabas across Cyprus and into several cities in southern Galatia (Acts 13–14).

After the Jerusalem Conference (Acts 15:1-35), Paul and Silas set off from Antioch on Paul's "second missionary journey" to revisit the young churches (Acts 15:36–16:5). They traveled east to west across southern Galatia, along the way adding Timothy to their team (Acts 16:1-5). Prevented by the Spirit from turning left, toward the province of Asia, or turning right, toward Bithynia, the team continued westward to Troas where Paul's vision of a man from Macedonia provided divine guidance (Acts 16:6-10). ("We" in Acts 16:10 probably indicates that Luke, the author of Acts, also joined the team.)

The missionary band then crossed the Aegean Sea and traveled along the major east-west overland route, the Egnatian Way. In Philippi, Thessalonica, and Berea, their experiences followed the same pattern: preaching in the synagogue, some coming to believe, a church beginning to form, opposition arising, and the team being forced to move on (Acts 16:11–17:15). Leaving Silas and Timothy behind in Berea, Paul traveled south into the province of Achaia—first to Athens, where there was limited response to his message, and then on to Corinth (Acts 17:16–18:4). There was opposition there, too, but, commanded by the Lord in a vision (Acts 18:9-10), Paul continued there for upward of two years (Acts 18:5-18a). Finally, he completed his second missionary journey by returning to Antioch via Jerusalem (Acts 18:18b-22).

Paul was the leader in this missionary activity, but clearly he was very much a team player. Colleagues played significant roles at various points. Luke probably stayed on at Philippi, since the use of "we" discontinues at that point, and is not resumed until 20:6. Silas and Timothy stayed on at Macedonia for a time (Acts 17:14) before joining Paul at Corinth (Acts 18:5). Their close partnership is shown by Paul's associating Silas and Timothy with himself as somehow sharing in the writing of both Thessalonian letters (1 Thess. 1:1).

Like the first letter, 2 Thessalonians claims (1:1; see also 3:17) to have been written by the Apostle Paul. He acknowledges some participation, not clearly defined, by Silas and Timothy, who were his colleagues on the missionary team which founded the church in Thessalonica in the course of Paul's second missionary journey (Acts 15:36–18:22, especially 15:40; 16:1-4; 17:1-9). The similarity of vocabulary and style between the two Thessalonian letters seems to confirm this judgment, which is attested by several early church fathers who were, of course, much closer to the situation than we, and who were fully capable of detecting forgeries.

RECIPIENTS

First Thessalonians was directed to the new Christian congregation in Thessalonica, which was a large and prosperous city, strategically located on the major east-west land route and at the junction of a highway north to the Danube region. It had the best natural harbor on the Aegean. Products from the surrounding fertile farmlands and forests helped to make the city important commercially.

As the capital of the province of Macedonia, Thessalonica was important politically. Because of its service to the Empire, Rome had designated it a "free city," which meant that it enjoyed limited self-government. For internal matters, five or six local officials called "politarchs" (the New International Version reads "city officials" [Acts 17:6, 8]) presided over a popular assembly of citizens. Other privileges included the authority to mint their own coins, freedom from housing Roman troops, and certain tax concessions. As would be expected in a commercial center, the population was mixed: mostly Greeks, with a number of Latin-speaking government people and merchants, and probably a significant Jewish population.

The founding of the church in Thessalonica is reported in Acts 17:1-9. Expelled from Philippi, Paul and his party traveled southwest along the Egnatian Way some one hundred miles to Thessalonica. Following their usual pattern in a new place, they began their ministry at the synagogue, where familiarity with the Old Testament would have prepared people for the message. Starting there was not a betrayal of Paul's mission to the Gentiles, because among those gathered in the synagogue would be a number of "God-fearers" (these were Gentiles attracted to the monotheism and high morality of Judaism, but not yet prepared to accept circumcision and become full-fledged members of the Jewish religious community[5]; for example, Cornelius in Acts 10). For the three Sabbaths that Paul was allowed to preach there, he proclaimed Jesus as Messiah. Some Jews and a larger number of Gentiles believed, including some upper-class women.

Jealous of their success, the synagogue leadership persuaded some local hoodlums to start a riot. Unable to locate Paul and Silas, they rounded up Jason, the householder where Paul was staying (Jason's home was perhaps the site of a house-church), along with some other local Christians, and brought them before the city officials, accusing them of harboring dangerous subversives. The charges were cleverly constructed: they accused Paul and Silas of being traveling agitators who defied Roman laws and treasonously called Jesus "King" (Acts 17:6-7). The city officials may have realized that the charges were false, but they would have been careful not to risk the special status of the city by even appearing to ignore disloyalty to Rome. And they needed to quiet the crowd.

Their solution was to require Jason and the other accused Christians to post bond to keep the peace, or perhaps to restrain the preaching activities of their missionary guests. This meant that Jason and friends would be responsible for any further commotion. This strategy tied the hands of the evangelists, since further ministry would endanger the local Christians more than themselves. The new Christians also urged them to move on (Acts 17:10a).

The missionary team went on to Berea and started in the synagogue once more. They had a better hearing there, but Jewish leaders from Thessalonica learned of it, and used the same methods as before to drive Paul out of Berea, too (Acts 17:10-15).

It is not clear how long Paul and company ministered in Thessalonica, but probably longer than the three Sabbaths mentioned in Acts 17:2. There are several indications of a longer stay: most of their converts were *pagan* Gentiles, not "God-fearers" from the synagogue (see 1 Thessalonians 1:9); they had served there long enough for the people to observe their lives (see 1 Thessalonians 1:5); and the congregation in Philippi had time to send offerings more than once (see Philippians 4:16).

First Thessalonians, then, was addressed to the young church in Thessalonica. The church had received some weeks of instruction in the things of Christ, but their founding pastor and his colleagues had been compelled to leave them abruptly, probably before they had been able to ground the church thoroughly in the faith. There is general agreement that this letter was written in A.D. 50 or 51, probably fairly early in the course of Paul's ministry at Corinth.

This commentary takes the persons addressed in 2 Thessalonians to be essentially the same congregation as that to which the first letter was written. A few scholars have sought to make a case for the view that the two letters were addressed to different segments within one overall congregation at Thessalonica, perhaps one group largely Jewish in background and the other Gentile. But if there had been a division in the Thessalonian church so significant that different letters were required for the two segments, it is incredible that Paul would not have addressed the matter directly, concerned as he was about the unity of the body of Christ, especially as between Jewish and Gentile Christians (see Ephesians 2:11-22;

Romans 11:13-32; 15:5-13; 25-27; also 1 Corinthians 12:12-13, 27). Had Paul felt the need to address the issue of unity, a passage like 2 Thessalonians 2:13-17 would have provided an appropriate context for treating the topic.

OCCASION/PURPOSE

During his second missionary journey, Paul went from Berea to Athens, where he did some preaching, but with only limited success (see Acts 17:16-34). Apparently, Timothy joined him there, but Paul sent him back to Thessalonica to see how things were going (see 1 Thessalonians 3:2, 5). Silas's whereabouts at this time are unknown; perhaps he was sent to Philippi.

Paul went on to Corinth, joined Aquila and Priscilla in their tent-making business, and was doing some synagogue preaching (Acts 18:1-4). According to Acts 18:5, both Silas and Timothy went to Corinth from Macedonia. They may have taken with them financial gifts, because verse 5 indicates that after their arrival, for a time at least, Paul could devote himself to full-time evangelism.

Timothy's report concerning the situation in the church at Thessalonica was, on the whole, very encouraging (1 Thess. 3:6-9). Paul's deep concerns (3:5) were relieved, and Timothy's good report was a breath of life to him (3:8). At the same time, there were some deficiencies (3:10). Timothy may have brought a letter from the Thessalonians asking questions. Timothy's report, then, is the occasion of 1 Thessalonians; it prompted Paul on one hand to give thanks for good news, and on the other hand to take steps dealing with matters which required attention.

Ordinarily, Paul had at least three options in dealing with problems in a distant church: he could make a personal visit (see 1 Corinthians 4:19; 16:5; 2 Corinthians 13:1-2); he could send a personal representative (see 1 Corinthians 4:17; 2 Corinthians 8:17-23; Ephesians 6:21-22); or he could send a letter (see 2 Corinthians 2:3; 13:10; Colossians 4:16).

Paul strongly affirmed in 1 Thessalonians 2:17-18 that he had wanted to make a personal visit to Thessalonica, but that Satan had blocked the way. Therefore, Paul had sent Timothy (1 Thess. 3:1-2, 5), who had returned with his report. Apparently, Paul still could not go to Thessalonica in person. The best he could do was write a letter. There is no indication who the bearer would be.

So, the *occasion*—the immediate situation which prompted the writing of 1 Thessalonians—was Timothy's report. But what were Paul's *purposes?*

Sometimes an author openly declares his primary purpose (for example, John 20:31; 1 John 5:13; 1 Peter 5:12), but more often we must deduce his purpose(s) from the contents of the letter. In the case of 1 Thessalonians, we may judge that Paul's purposes included encouragement in continuing persecution (especially 1 Thessalonians 1:1-10; 2:13-16; 3:6-13); response to slanders against Paul's ministry (2:1-12); rebuke for laxness on sexual morality (4:1-8); relieving concern about deceased Christians in relation to the Second Coming (4:13-18); reassurance concerning the return of Christ (5:1-11); and dealing with several minor problems—working to support themselves, respect for leaders, suppressing spiritual gifts, and the need for harmony and mutual helpfulness (4:9-12; 5:12-22).

Throughout the letter, there is the note of joy and pride Paul felt as their spiritual father, together with loving concern for their continued progress in the midst of an unfriendly environment. In spite of the limited time their teachers had been able to spend with the church, apparently Paul felt no need for extended instruction in doctrine, except for some clarifications concerning the second coming of Christ.

Above all, he revealed his pastoral heart. As F. F. Bruce puts it, "Paul reveals himself in every sentence of this letter as a true and faithful pastor, rejoicing in his flock but anxious for their welfare, confident and concerned, thanking God for them and simultaneously praying to God for them, tirelessly caring for them as a father for his children, straining his strength to the limit in order not to be a burden to them."[6]

The result is a letter which John Wesley found especially "sweet." He said of it, "There is a peculiar sweetness in this epistle, unmixed with any sharpness or reproof; those evils which the apostles afterward reproved not yet having crept into the church."[7]

A few New Testament scholars have taken the view that the relation between the two Thessalonian letters is better explained if 2 Thessalonians is taken to be the earlier of the two (recently argued at considerable length by Charles Wanamaker[8]). The issue is complex (see, for example, Ernest Best[9]). Without reviewing the argument here, this commentary will follow those who maintain the traditional order.

Nowhere in 2 Thessalonians is there a clear-cut and definitive statement of the author's purpose; nothing comparable to 1 Timothy 3:14-15, for example. But even if the author does not spell out his motivation in so many words, usually the contents of the letter provide clues to his concerns. When both letters to the Thessalonians are scrutinized in a search for the author's purpose, it soon becomes apparent that there is considerable overlapping of topics between the two.

In the first letter, Paul and his colleagues begin with an expression of gratitude to God for the Thessalonians' response to the gospel in spite of persecution; they then review their ministry on the founding visit; and Paul next reports his joyful reaction to Timothy's report concerning his return visit to the Thessalonians, then closes the first main division with prayer in their behalf. The second main division exhorts the new Christians to appropriate lifestyle in their community, especially to sexual purity; it then provides further explanation concerning the return of Christ in relation to both the dead in Christ and the living, and concludes with instructions concerning congregational life and work, and a final prayer.

In the second letter, Paul and his colleagues no longer think it necessary to defend the character of their ministry among the Thessalonians, nor to deal further with issues of sexual morality, but otherwise the topics are familiar. The converts still needed encouragement because of continuing persecution, further explanation concerning the return of Christ, and stricter instructions for dealing with problems in community life, particularly with some members who persisted in being idlers.

The second letter zeroes in on these topics and, incidentally, does so in a manner which confirms the view that this letter is the later of the two. D. E. Hiebert cites William Neil: "In each of the topics dealt with—persecution, Second Advent, idleness—there is an obvious intensification of the difficulties and development of the situation, as described in the first letter, which makes any alteration of sequence impossible."[10] Thus the letter is sometimes described as a second prescription for a condition in which certain stubborn symptoms were still persisting.

We do not have the kind of background information which the book of Acts provides for the first letter, but the close similarity between the two letters suggests that the second was written not long after the first. Paul's ministry at Corinth was a fairly lengthy one—a year and a half, according to Acts 18:11. Almost certainly Paul and his colleagues were still laboring there when this letter was written, probably about A.D. 51. We do not know how the missionaries became aware of the continuing problems; perhaps the bearer of 1 Thessalonians returned and reported on the situation. Nor do we know who carried this letter to its intended readers.

We conclude, then, that three particular problems prompted a second letter to the Thessalonian congregation: (1) continuing, perhaps intensifying, persecution; (2) further concern and confusion about Christ's Return, but now with a new focus provoked by some stimulus the exact nature of which is unknown to Paul (2 Thess. 2:2); and (3) perhaps because of end-time excitement, some converts had discontinued working and apparently were living on the generosity of other Christians. As in the first letter, at several points Paul breaks into prayer for them, much of it in the nature of thanksgiving, and he also asks them to pray for him because of continued dangers and obstacles he and his colleagues are experiencing.

In summary, then, the *occasion* which prompted 2 Thessalonians was information, received by letter and/or oral report (3:11), indicating the persistence of certain problems. Its *purpose* was to encourage in continuing persecution, to instruct concerning the second coming of Christ, and to admonish the congregation to deal with idlers in their midst. And the letter comes permeated with the love and prayers of its writers.

ENDNOTES

[1]Leander E. Keck and Victor Paul Furnish, *The Pauline Letters* (Nashville: Abingdon Press, 1984), p. 16. Italics added.

[2]Leon Morris, *The First and Second Epistles to the Thessalonians,* New International Commentary on the New Testament (Grand Rapids, Michigan: Wm. B. Eerdmans Publishing Co., 1991), pp. 15–23.

[3]I. Howard Marshall, *1 and 2 Thessalonians*, New Century Bible Commentary (Grand Rapids, Michigan: Wm. B. Eerdmans Publishing Co., 1983), pp. 23–45.

[4]Often Paul's three years in "Arabia" (see Galatians 1:17) have been thought of as a period of quiet reflection on the personal and theological significance of his Damascus Road encounter with Christ. But Acts 9:20 describes him as beginning to preach in the synagogues of Damascus "at once." We should note that "Arabia" designates not just the region of modern Arabia, but the Nabatean Kingdom, ruled by King Aretas IV, which apparently bordered or even included Damascus. That Paul did not spend all his time in private meditation is demonstrated by the fact that his preaching activities were successful enough to cause King Aretas's governor to seek his arrest (see 2 Corinthians 11:32-33) and to cause the Jews of Damascus to conspire to kill him (see Acts 9:23).

[4]Monotheism is the belief that there is only one God. The life and belief system of the Jewish people (Judaism) involves a covenant relationship with God, and though there are various branches of Judaism, the underlying theme among them has been monotheism and a recognition of the Law, or the Torah. The Hebrew word from which *Torah* comes is translated *law* and refers to divine instruction and guidance. The Torah is comprised of the instructions and directions given to Israel by God. Torah is another name for the Pentateuch (the first five books of the Old Testament: Genesis, Exodus, Leviticus, Numbers, and Deuteronomy), also known as the Law of Moses. It is considered the most important division in the Jewish Scriptures, with highest authority, since it was traditionally thought to have been written by Moses, the only biblical hero to have spoken with God face-to-face.

⁶F. F. Bruce in "1 and 2 Thessalonians," D. Guthrie and J. A. Motyer, eds., *New Bible Commentary,* rev. ed. (Grand Rapids, Michigan: Wm. B. Eerdmans Co., 1970), p. 1155.

⁷John Wesley, *Explanatory Notes upon the New Testament* (London: Epworth Press, 1950), p. 754.

⁸Charles A. Wanamaker, *The Epistles to the Thessalonians,* New International Greek Testament Commentary (Grand Rapids, Michigan: Wm. B. Eerdmans Publishing Co., 1990), pp. 37–45.

⁹Ernest Best, *A Commentary on the First and Second Epistles to the Thessalonians,* Harper's New Testament Commentaries (New York: Harper and Row Publishers, 1972), pp. 42–45.

¹⁰D. E. Hiebert, *The Thessalonian Epistles* (Chicago: Moody Press, 1971), p. 270.

1 THESSALONIANS OUTLINE

I. **THE THESSALONIAN CHURCH: PAST AND PRESENT (1:1–3:13)**
  A. **Past: First Visit (1:1–2:16)**
    1. 1:1   Address
    2. 1:2-10   Thanksgiving for the Thessalonians' Response
      a. 1:2-7   Their Conversion
      b. 1:8-10 Their Witness
    3. 2:1-12   Defense of the Ministry
    4. 2:13-16 Further Thanks for the Thessalonians' Response
  B. **Present: Timothy's Visit (2:17–3:13)**
    1. 2:17-20 Paul's Return Prevented
    2. 3:1-5   Timothy Sent
    3. 3:6-10   Timothy's Report
    4. 3:11-13 Prayer for the Thessalonians' Growth

II. **THE THESSALONIAN CHURCH: PRESENT AND FUTURE (4:1–5:28)**
  A. **Present: Practical Holiness (4:1-12)**
    1. 4:1-2   Instructions Given
    2. 4:3-8   Sexual Purity
    3. 4:9-12   Christian Community
  B. **Future: Return of Christ (4:13–5:11)**
    1. 4:13-18 Reassurance Concerning Deceased Christians
    2. 5:1-11   Assurance for the Living
  C. **Present: Congregational Duties (5:12-24)**
    1. 5:12-15 Social
    2. 5:16-22 Religious
    3. 5:23-24 Prayer for Sanctification
  D. **Conclusion (5:25-28)**
    1. 5:25-27 Closing Exhortations
    2. 5:28   Benediction

Part One

THE THESSALONIAN CHURCH: PAST AND PRESENT

1 Thessalonians 1:1–3:13

P aul and his missionary colleagues have important instructions, clarifications, and exhortations to convey to the young church in Thessalonica. Their original visit was cut short when they were compelled to leave the city (see Acts 17:5-10). Timothy may have had some opportunity for further teaching when he returned for the second visit, but now back in Corinth, he reports to Paul that the young church has made good progress in spite of continuing persecution (1 Thess. 3:6-9). Unable himself to travel to Thessalonica, Paul uses the only means of communication available to him—a letter which, we may assume, contains at least some of the teaching he would have given had he been among them (see also 3:10).

However, rather than launching immediately into instruction, Paul first reviews what has already happened in the life of the young church, and does it in such a way as to prepare them for the instruction he will give in 4:1 through 5:24. The chief way he strengthens rapport is by sharing with these recent converts the prayers of thanksgiving he and his colleagues have offered regularly to God, both for their initial response to the gospel and for their remaining faithful in spite of further persecution.

It is true that in most of his letters, Paul follows the opening words of address with thanksgiving, sometimes intermingled with prayer for the recipients, as in Romans 1:8-10; 1 Corinthians 1:4-9; Philippians 1:3-11; Colossians 1:3-14. Galatians is the notable exception.

However, 1 Thessalonians is unique among Paul's letters in that there is not only the lengthy thanksgiving at the beginning (1 Thess. 1:2-10), but there is another in 2:13-16, and still a third in 3:9-13. These are genuine prayers, offered to God to thank Him for the way He has been working in the lives of these recent converts. But the reason for telling the Thessalonians about these prayers is the hope that, as they "hear" these prayers offered on their behalf, they will be encouraged and motivated to continue in the life of faith they have begun.

Between the first and second of these thanksgivings, Paul defends the integrity of his and his colleagues' ministry among the Thessalonians (2:1-12). This note is sounded briefly in 1:5, but in 2:1-12, it is expanded to a more detailed refutation of a series of implied accusations. Paul's purpose is not so much self-vindication as to prevent these misrepresentations from undermining the confidence of the recent converts.

And between the second and third thanksgivings, Paul reassures the Thessalonians concerning his love for them (2:17–3:5); describes his frustration at being stopped from getting back to Thessalonica for a follow-up visit (2:18; 3:1); tells them of the decision to send Timothy (3:1-5); and expresses his delight at Timothy's good report (3:6-8). And this prompts the third thanksgiving (3:9-10).

Paul has been a father in God to these people (2:11), and he would love to have a family reunion (2:17). That being impossible at the time, he opens his heart to them in this letter. In the first main division, he remembers their initial response to the gospel (1:1-10); defends the integrity of his and his colleagues' ministry among them (2:1-12); encourages them in the ongoing persecution (2:13-16); explains why he sent Timothy in his stead (2:17–3:5); describes his joy at their progress (3:5-10); and finally rises to a crescendo of prayer on their behalf (3:11-13). He then believes the atmosphere to be right for the other side of his fatherly role—moral instruction (4:1–5:24).

PAST: FIRST VISIT

1 Thessalonians 1:1–2:16

A fter greeting the Thessalonians in the manner customary in those days, Paul and his colleagues begin by remembering their ministry there. Two topics are intertwined: (1) the missionaries' ministry and (2) the Thessalonians' response. In the letter's first section (1:1-10), the missionaries celebrate the Thessalonians' profound response to the gospel in both personal commitment (1:2-3, 6) and effective witness (1:7-9). They also recall the way the Holy Spirit has enabled them to preach powerfully and live consistently in the Thessalonians' midst (1:4-6).

The second section of the letter (2:1-16) continues both themes, but the emphasis is reversed. In 1:1-10, the Thessalonians' response receives the greater stress, but in 2:1-16, the emphasis lies in describing the missionaries' ministry in Thessalonica in such a way as to reveal their integrity before God and man (2:1-12). And there is also further recognition of the young church's steadfastness even under persecution (2:13-16).

1. ADDRESS 1:1

Paul addresses the Thessalonian church in accordance with the standard procedure for letter writing at that time. The usual order was (1) the introduction of the writer(s); (2) the naming of the recipient(s); and (3) a greeting, frequently followed by a prayer for the health and prosperity of the readers. Paul includes Silas and Timothy in his introduction because they were part of the missionary team when the church was founded, and they are with him at Corinth when this letter is being written. Indeed, one of them may be the scribe taking down the letter (notice the statement in 2 Thessalonians 3:17 identifying Paul as the writer of the final greeting).

It is difficult to determine precisely the degree of Silas's and Timothy's participation in the actual writing of the letter. The use of "we" (1:2) continues rather consistently throughout the letter, with 2:18; 3:5; and 5:27 being the only exceptions. This contrasts with 1 Corinthians, which is more typical of Paul's letters. There Paul begins with "Paul . . . and our brother Sosthenes," but then immediately, in 1:4, he prays, "I always thank God for you. . . ," and the letter continues mostly with the singular "I."

In this letter to the Thessalonians, the exceptions just mentioned— 2:18; 3:5; 5:27—may be the evidence that, at bottom, the mind and heart behind the Thessalonian letters are, in the first instance, the Apostle Paul's. But at the same time, the colleagues who worked closely with him then in Thessalonica and now in Corinth share profoundly in the ideas and feelings expressed. That assurance will encourage the Thessalonian Christians.

Silas (1:1; also known as Sylvanus) was identified as a "leader among the brothers" and "a prophet" (see Acts 15:22, 32) when he was ministering in the church at Antioch. Selected by Paul after the departure of Barnabas (Acts 15:40), apparently Silas traveled with Paul throughout the second missionary journey. His last mention as a coworker with Paul is in 2 Corinthians 1:19. Most scholars identify him with the Silas later named as an associate of Peter (see 1 Peter 5:12).

Converted under Paul's ministry in the course of the first missionary journey (see 1 Corinthians 4:17; 1 Timothy 1:2), **Timothy** (1 Thess. 1:1) joined the missionary team during the second journey (Acts 16:1-4) and seems to have served as a trusted junior colleague throughout the rest of Paul's missionary career (see Acts 19:22; Romans 16:21; 1 Corinthians 4:17; 16:10; 2 Corinthians 1:19; Philippians 2:19-23). He was with Paul during his first Roman imprisonment (Phil. 1:1), and was called back to Rome in the course of Paul's final imprisonment (2 Tim. 4:9-13). He is probably the Timothy of Hebrews 13:23.

Silas and Timothy are just two of the very substantial number, both men and women, named as Paul's colleagues in ministry, to one degree or another, in Acts and in Paul's various letters. This indicates one of the aspects of Paul's ministry. E. E. Ellis affirms that "some one hundred individuals, under a score of titles and activities, are associated with the apostle at one time or another during his ministry. . . ." Ellis further states that "thirty-six coworkers under nine designations can be identified with considerable probability."[1] Paul was a team player.

The letter before us is directed to **the church of the Thessalonians** (1 Thess. 1:1). The word translated **church** appears frequently in the Greek Old Testament (called the Septuagint[2]) for the people of Israel as the special people of God, especially when they were assembled in His presence. William Barclay summarizes the meaning of the term as used in the New Testament: "In essence, therefore, the Church . . . is a body of people, not so much assembling because they have chosen to come together, but assembling because God has called them to Himself; not so much assembling to share their own thoughts and opinions, but assembling to listen to the voice of God."[3]

Whether or not all those historical associations were uppermost in his mind at the moment, Paul writes with the expectation that, when the news circulates that his letter has arrived, the Thessalonian congregation will gather promptly. Whether in one large assembly or, more likely, in their several house-churches, they will hear someone read aloud to them the letter from their beloved apostle (5:27; see 2 Thessalonians 3:14).

The Thessalonian believers are further described as being **in God the Father and the Lord Jesus Christ** (1 Thess. 1:1). This distinguishes their gathering from all other assemblies, religious or secular, which might exist in Thessalonica. But, more profoundly, the little preposition **in** indicates the Source of their true identity as the people of God. It points to a vital, life-giving union (see John 15:4; 2 Corinthians 5:17).

Another significant detail: we should notice how the phrases **God the Father** and **Lord Jesus Christ** are placed side by side and under the single preposition **in** (1 Thess. 1:1). This tends to put them on the same level and, thus, implies Jesus' deity. **Lord** is used in both Testaments in a very considerable range of meanings, from "sir" to an address to deity. But its use regularly in the Greek Old Testament to translate YAHWEH, and the immediate context here, also point to the acknowledgment of Christ's deity. This may be commonplace for us, but for someone like Paul—reared and educated in rigorous Jewish monotheism[4]—such language is another clear indication that his thought patterns have been transformed drastically in the light of his Damascus Road encounter with the risen Christ.

The greeting, **Grace and peace to you** (1:1), combines the *source* of blessing, **grace,** God's undeserved favor, and the *result* of that blessing, **peace.** And of course, in the Bible, **peace** is more than absence of conflict, more than personal inner tranquility. It is the New Testament equivalent of the Hebrew *Shalom,* and thus signifies wholeness, well-being in the highest sense (see Numbers 6:24-26). And it is not only individual, but also communal, transforming interpersonal relationships throughout the church, and extending to those around us who have not yet come to believe in Christ and, thus, experience His peace for themselves. It is what the Messiah would bring (see Isaiah 9:6-7; also Ephesians 2:14, 17; Colossians 1:20), and now Christians are to be its instrument (see Matthew 5:9).

Before leaving our consideration of these two foundational terms, we should note the important fact that they always appear in the same order—first grace, and then peace. In the words of Leon Morris, "There can be no true peace until the grace of God has dealt with sin."[5]

After the greeting, the next item in the conventional pattern of ancient letters was a thanksgiving and/or a prayer for the well-being of the readers, and, as we have seen, this is Paul's usual pattern. In 1 Thessalonians 1, he does proceed next to thanksgiving, but at once gets involved in a long train of thought describing their conversion, which runs clear through the end of the chapter (1:10). Later, he will remind them of the character of his ministry among them (2:1-12); then will express another thanksgiving (2:13-16); and, after speaking of Timothy's later visit (2:17–3:8), will burst forth with yet another expression of thanks (3:9-10).

2. THANKSGIVING FOR THE THESSALONIANS' RESPONSE 1:2-10

a. Their Conversion (1:2-7). The intensity and earnestness of the initial prayer of thanksgiving here are conspicuous. We often think of Paul as preacher, evangelist, church planter and, eventually, martyr, but less often as prayer warrior and constant intercessor. We may hardly notice a passage like 2 Corinthians 11:28-29, which vividly illustrates the depth of feeling characterizing Paul's pastoral concern. It is likely that the **we** of 1 Thessalonians 1:2-7 includes Silas and Timothy and, for that matter, perhaps Priscilla and Aquila, along with other Christians at Corinth. But Paul takes the lead and assures the congregation that the prayers of these include **all** the believers in Thessalonica (1:2). He will be careful to make the same point in 5:26-27 (twice).

It is not evident in English versions, but in the Greek text **thank** (1:2) is expanded by three action verbs which spell out more fully the length and breadth of the missionaries' prayer concern: **mentioning** (1:2); **remembering** (1:3); and **knowing** (1:4). Their prayers regularly name the Thessalonian Christians, remember their growth in grace, and rejoice in the knowledge that God has chosen them to be His own. The form of the Greek verb here translated **mentioning** implies regular, repeated activity (notice the **always**), and this is reinforced by describing the remembering as taking place **continually** (1:3). The Thessalonians are often in the missionaries' thoughts and intercessions, as Paul and his colleagues do their praying, live out their lives, and carry on their ministry **before our God and Father** (1:3).

In particular, Paul thanks God for a triad of virtues evident in the lives of the Thessalonian Christians: **faith, love,** and **hope** (1:3; this is a common grouping in the New Testament, though not always in the same order, as in 1 Thessalonians 5:8; 1 Corinthians 13:13; Colossians 1:5; see also Galatians 5:5-6; Ephesians 4:2-5; Hebrews 6:10-12; 10:22-24; 1 Peter 1:21-22).

Faith, love, hope (1 Thess. 1:3): all three are, in the first instance, God's good gifts (see 1 Corinthians 12:9; 1 Thessalonians 4:9; Romans 15:13), but they are also habits of the heart which we are called upon to develop and exercise. As we do, they become productive in our lives. In the words of Ernest Best, "In the present passage each of the triad is qualified by a word which suggests activity; the triad thus does not consist of three virtues to be contemplated but three to be expressed."[6]

Faith works; **love** labors; **hope** endures. **Faith** is more than intellectual; it is total, personal commitment to Christ which leads to action. **Love** labors, and the word is a strong one, implying painful, persistent effort. So, if faith works; love is prepared even to toil; it never wearies of serving those who are loved (Gal. 5:6). Ernest Best comments that their love is to imitate God's (1 Thess. 1:6) and is, therefore, inclusive. And he adds, "This love is neither a mere warmth of heart toward others, for many have to be loved who have nothing about them which would arouse affection, nor is it to be devoid of warmth, for then it would become a burden."[7]

And that persistent labor of love is sustained in an **endurance** which is **inspired by hope** (1:3). And hope in the New Testament is not just a general optimism about the future based on human speculation. It has a solid foundation of confidence in God, based on what He has done in Christ (Rom. 5:1-5; 1 Cor. 15:19-28; Col. 1:27; Heb. 6:19-20; 1 Pet. 1:3, 21). The power of hope to inspire endurance is being exhibited in the lives of the Thessalonians as they persevere even under persecution.

Paul now uses his favorite term for fellow Christians, one which is scattered throughout his letters—**brothers** (1 Thess. 1:4). It is found twenty-one times in the two short Thessalonian letters, plus another seven times in the singular form. (Sisters are included of course, although, in accordance with the custom of the times, they are not explicitly named.)

The term **brothers** was widely used at that time by both Jews and Gentiles, not only for blood relatives, but also for fellow religionists and fellow members of secular societies, such as trade guilds. Found in every New Testament writing except Jude and 2 John, its Christian usage goes directly back to Jesus (for example, Mark 3:34-35; 10:30; Matthew 25:40). It is the natural consequence of regarding God as our common Father through the new birth (John 3:5-21) or adoption (Gal. 4:4-7; Rom. 8:14-17, 23). We are members of the same family, brothers and sisters (Mark 3:34; 2 Cor. 6:18; see also 1 Peter 2:17; 5:9). The practical implications are far-reaching in terms of both privilege and responsibility (Matt. 5:23-24; 7:3-5; 18:21-22; Luke 17:3-4; 1 Cor. 8:11-13).

Paul continues to be thankful now (1 Thess. 1:4) for the assurance that God **has chosen** the Thessalonian Christians. *Election* is the older theological term used for God's choice of His people, and historically it has been a controversial doctrine, though clearly taught in Scripture. Its roots are deeply embedded in the Old Testament where Israel is frequently described as God's chosen people (for example, Exodus 19:5-6). Jesus applies almost the same language to His disciples (John 15:16), as Peter does to the church (1 Pet. 2:9-10), and as God, speaking in a vision experience, does with reference to Paul himself (Acts 9:15).

The theological and practical value of the doctrine of election is its declaration that God is always previous in our salvation. He takes the initiative. Of course, our part is also necessary, but it always has the nature of response—in fact, a divinely enabled response (John 6:44, 65; 12:32; see also Jeremiah 31:3).

However, we must be clear that the biblical doctrine of election does not undermine the reality and seriousness of human responsibility. In fact, it makes us *more* accountable (see 2 Peter 1:10; Amos 3:2). In Scripture it is presented as a motive for obedience (see 1 Peter 1:2); for holy living (see Leviticus 20:7; Ephesians 1:4; Colossians 3:12); for Christlikeness (see Romans 8:29); for fruit bearing (see John 15:16); and for mission to the nations (see Acts 9:15; 1 Peter 2:9-10). That is to say that election is primarily being chosen for responsibility, not just for privilege. So understood, the doctrine of election does not foster complacency, but stimulates active pursuit of God's will, impelled by love and gratitude. John Stott summarizes the New Testament use of the doctrine: "Moreover, the topic of election is nearly always introduced for a practical purpose, in order to foster assurance (not presumption), holiness (not moral apathy), humility (not pride) and witness (not lazy selfishness)."[8]

Why God chose us remains an ultimate mystery, except for the clue implied here in the words **loved by God** (1 Thess. 1:4). Very likely, Paul has in mind here some of the classical statements in the Old Testament, such as Deuteronomy 7:6-8, which echoes Deuteronomy 4:37 (also 10:15; 14:2; see Psalm 33:12). He loves because it is His nature to love, and not because we are all that lovable, nor even because of what He can make of us.

But how does Paul *know* that God has chosen the Thessalonian believers? In this immediate context, Paul offers two bits of evidence: (1) the way he and his colleagues were enabled to preach (1 Thess. 1:5) and (2) the way the Thessalonians responded (1:6-7).

The missionaries call the message they preached **our gospel** (1:5), "ours" not in the sense that they own or control it. In fact, its Author owns *them;* they are His ambassadors, and He has spoken through them (2 Cor. 5:20). Therefore the message **came . . . with power** (1 Thess. 1:5), power in the lives of both the evangelists and the hearers. In this case, the evangelistic team experienced the unction of the Holy Spirit to an unusual degree, enabling them to preach with **power** and **conviction.** The construction of the Greek text persuades most scholars that **conviction** here (1:5) refers to the manner of the missionaries' preaching, and not to the Thessalonians' reaction. In their Thessalonian mission, the speakers experienced such a degree of fervency that they were sure God meant to do something in the community.

Another aspect of the missionaries' ministry there is mentioned almost parenthetically: **You know how we lived among you for your sake** (1:5b). The character and conduct of the missionary team was consistent with their message. Their words and deeds pointed in the same direction. Recent high-profile scandals among American televangelists have vividly illustrated how crucial this is. It will be dealt with more fully in 1 Thessalonians 2:1-12.

In 1:6, Paul indicates the second proof that God has chosen the Thessalonians—the way they were enabled to respond. He begins, **You became imitators of us and of the Lord** (1:6a). This imitation theme has Old Testament precedent (Lev. 19:2), and the idea appears several times in the New Testament (Matt. 5:48; Luke 6:36; 1 Pet. 1:16). Most New Testament scholars think that when the term **Lord** (1 Thess. 1:6) stands by itself in the Pauline writings, the reference is to Jesus rather than to God the Father. Thus, the meaning is "You became imitators of Jesus." That interpretation is appropriate in this context; we remember how Jesus called His people to follow Him (Mark 8:34; John 13:15; see also 1 Peter 2:21; 1 John 2:6).

Of course, here in 1 Thessalonians 1:6, Paul also refers to himself (and his colleagues) as a model to young Christians. He does so elsewhere more emphatically (see Philippians 3:17; 1 Corinthians 4:16; 11:1). This is not presumptuous on his part; it simply follows from his clear conscience. He believes that his life is consistent with his message. Certainly we would not wish him to do the opposite—to say, "Do as I say, and not as I do." And if we are surprised at his mentioning himself first— **imitators of us and of the Lord** (1 Thess. 1:6)—we might remember that this is the order of experience in a pioneer missionary situation. Before the message of the missionary is understood or accepted, the people will have been observing his or her life.

We need to remember also that at this point in time, although some of the information now contained in the Gospels was available to the Thessalonians, neither the written Gospels nor the other Epistles (of which the Thessalonian letters are a part) were available to them.[9] The Thessalonians could not turn to these writings for guidance, as we so readily can. It may not be off the mark to observe that, in spite of the abundance of Scripture versions readily available to us, with respect to accurate knowledge of the life and teachings of Jesus and of the apostles, many traditionally Christian nations like our own are becoming more like "mission fields." Therefore, the need for Christians to model the message is urgent.

Paul continues to give evidence that God has chosen the Thessalonians and is at work in their lives: they have **welcomed the message,** received it warmly and hospitably, given it room in their hearts; and they have exhibited **joy given by the Holy Spirit** (1:6). This is the second mention of the Spirit in this immediate context; first, He enabled the evangelists to preach effectively (1:5), and then He enabled the hearers to receive the word into their lives joyfully **in spite of severe suffering** (1:6).

Though remote from the lives of most North Americans (with individual exceptions, of course), **suffering** (or, perhaps better, "tribulation") was almost the norm in early Christian experience (1 Thess. 3:4; 2 Thess. 1:4-5; Rom. 5:3; 2 Cor. 1:5-6; Phil. 1:29; 3:10; 1 Pet. 1:6; 2:21; 5:9-10). Among Jesus' last words to His followers, just before leaving the Upper Room, was the warning, "In this world you will have trouble. But take heart! I have overcome the world" (John 16:33). In the case of the Thessalonians, an evidence of God's being at work in their lives is their joyful acceptance of the gospel message and their stalwart perseverance in spite of severe hardship. Ernest Best remarks that this is "not joy which comes at the end of suffering as its reward, but one which accompanies the suffering itself and upholds the sufferer in his suffering."[10]

We have no detailed knowledge of what hardships the Thessalonians experienced, but certainly the forces that succeeded in getting rid of the missionary team would next focus on the local believers, who were probably in a vulnerable position. The only explanation for their continued joy, Paul affirms, is that this is the fruit of the Holy Spirit in their lives (Gal. 5:22; Acts 5:41; 16:25; Phil. 1:29; 1 Pet. 4:13).

It may be legitimate to raise the question, if tribulation is the context for *normal* Christian living, is it only a matter of time until we are back to "normality"? Or is our Christianity so diluted that it no longer threatens the existing state of affairs? Are we no longer dangerous?

Further evidence of the Thessalonians' choice by God and additional cause for thanksgiving is given in 1 Thessalonians 1:7. In the Greek, this sentence is connected with verse 6 as expressing result: *so that* **you became a model.** They have been following the examples of Jesus and of Paul so closely that they themselves have become **a model to all the believers in Macedonia and Achaia** (1:7). The word translated **model** can mean a "pattern" (Acts 7:44) or "example" (1 Tim. 4:12; Phil. 3:17; 2 Thess. 3:9; Titus 2:7; 1 Pet. 5:3) from which observers may learn. That Paul says **model** (singular) suggests that he is referring to the communal life of the church.

According to the record in Acts, by the time of this writing there were churches in Philippi, Berea, Athens, and Corinth, and very probably the witness had also spread into the surrounding towns and villages (such as Cenchrea, near Corinth; Rom. 16:1). We are not to take the **all** (1:7; or the "everywhere" in verse 8) literally; the intention is to emphasize the broad scope of the witness of this young church and its widespread impact. We may compare this to the way we are encouraged today by reports of what the Lord is doing in some far-off mission situation.

b. Their Witness (1:8-10). In the Greek text of 1 Thessalonians 1:8, the use of the word "for" (omitted by the New International Version) indicates that Paul is explaining further how the Thessalonians have been a good "model" (1:7) in the effect of their conversion upon others. The spreading news includes both **the Lord's message** (1:8; literally, "the word of the Lord" or the gospel) and the Thessalonians' response to it. The **message rang out** (1:8). The Greek word for **rang out** is a strong one; early commentators compared it to the sound of a trumpet or a clap of thunder. And the form of the verb suggests that it did ring out and continues to ring. Indeed, for those with ears to hear, the testimony of the Thessalonian Christians continues to sound from the pages of holy Scripture.

As for the original sounding forth, there would have been many travelers coming and going to and through Thessalonica, since it was a port city, a junction for major roads, a commercial center and provincial headquarters. I. Howard Marshall points out that it "was very likely that Christians from other towns in Macedonia would visit [Thessalonica]. They would be glad of hospitality from local Christians, since in the ancient world it was difficult to get decent accommodation."[11]

Priscilla and Aquila had recently come from Rome (see Acts 18:2), and they may have informed Paul that even there people were talking about the success of the gospel in Thessalonica. In any case, as Paul and his colleagues traveled about, they found that reports concerning the Thessalonians had preceded them. Later Paul would make use of the widely known reputation of the Macedonian churches as an example to spur other Christians to generous giving (see 2 Corinthians 8:1-5; Macedonia was the province in which Thessalonica was located).

First Thessalonians 1:9-10 describes the **reception** the Thessalonian believers had given the ministry of Paul and his colleagues. This brief passage is of special interest for the clues it provides concerning the content of early missionary preaching and teaching. The statement is concise, but careful consideration of the language here reveals profound implications. A great deal of theology is packed into these few words.

If we carefully unpack what is said here, we will find materials for building a doctrine of God. His uniqueness is implied; in the Greek He is **the** God (1:9). He is further described as **living and true** (1:9; see also Jeremiah 10:10), in contrast to idols and false gods (see Acts 17:29; 1 Corinthians 8:4; 1 John 5:21). He reveals himself as the God and Father of **his Son . . . Jesus** (1 Thess. 1:10; see also 1 John 4:9) by raising Jesus **from the dead** (1 Thess. 1:10; see also Acts 3:15; 13:30) and exalting Him to His present position in **heaven** (1 Thess. 1:10; see also Philippians 2:9-11). And the reference to the **coming wrath** (1 Thess. 1:10; see also John 3:36; Ephesians 5:6; Colossians 3:6) points to God as the righteous Judge of all the earth (see Romans 2:5-11).

The doctrine of the wrath of God is difficult to keep in proper balance. Perhaps I. Howard Marshall has it right when he says, "It is perfectly consistent for God to display his holy and righteous character by judging sinners if they persist in their sin, and at the same time by loving them to the limit in giving his Son to be their Saviour from sin and its consequences."[12]

Significant elements for a strong doctrine of Christ are also stated or implied here. Concerning the Person of Christ, the name **Jesus** (1 Thess. 1:10; see also Matthew 1:21) is a pointer to His humanity (Phil. 2:5-8). It identifies Him with Jesus of Nazareth and thus implies the Incarnation (John 1:14).[13] On the other hand, the designation **Son** (1 Thess. 1:10; see also Matthew 3:17; 17:5) points to His oneness in nature with His Father in heaven and thus implies His deity (John 5:18; 14:9; Col. 2:9). This is confirmed by His being **raised from the dead** (1 Thess. 1:10; see also Romans 1:3-4; Galatians 1:1; 1 Peter 1:21). His ascension is indicated by the reference to His presence in **heaven** (1 Thess. 1:10; see also John 16:28; Acts 7:56; Colossians 3:1), and His second coming by the fact that believers **wait** (1 Thess. 1:10; see also 1 Corinthians 1:7; Philippians 3:20; Romans 8:19) for Him to come **from heaven** (1 Thess. 1:10; see also Acts 1:11).

Christ's saving work is clearly affirmed by the word **rescues** (1 Thess. 1:10; see also John 3:17; Galatians 3:13; 4:4-5; Romans 7:24; Colossians 1:13; Hebrews 9:28). Furthermore, **rescues** suggests that Christ's saving work is an ongoing process; its culmination will be our acquittal at the bar of God's judgment when, for Christ's sake, we are delivered **from the coming wrath** (1 Thess. 1:10; see also 5:9).

One can also deduce from this passage a capsule statement concerning the Christian life. It began when we **turned to God** (1 Thess. 1:9; see also Acts 3:19; 14:15); continues as we **serve the living and true God** (1 Thess. 1:9); and reaches its goal at the return of Christ for whom we **wait** (1:10). Thus, it begins with conversion, but that turnaround is just the beginning. **Turned** implies the embracing of a whole new perspective. Leon Morris quotes F. V. Filson: "In government, religion, business, amusement, labor and social clubs the pagan world was built on the pattern of polytheism [acknowledgement of a number of gods] . . . whereas the attitude of Apostolic Christianity to the polytheistic world was one of militant hostility."[14] Paul warned Corinthian Christians of the danger of participation in such activities, even by those who thought themselves sophisticated enough to be able to participate without being harmed (1 Cor. 8:1-13; 10:14-22).

In our time, John Stott warns concerning modern idols, "Some people are eaten up with a selfish ambition for money, power or fame. Others are obsessed with their work, or with sport or television, or are infatuated with a person or addicted to food, alcohol, hard drugs or sex. Both immorality and greed are later pronounced by Paul to be forms of idolatry, because they demand an allegiance which is due to God alone."[15]

But the turning which is Christian conversion is not only negative, **from idols;** positively, we turn in order **to serve** (1 Thess. 1:9). The Greek-English dictionary defines the word translated **serve** as "to perform the duties of a slave, serve, obey."[16] The Christian life is that of a person who knows that he is *owned*. He has been "bought at a price" (1 Cor. 6:20). But at the same time, it is a life that is free and fulfilling, the life for which we were created. It is, in the fullest sense, living *naturally*. We experience the gospel transformation: "You are no longer a slave, but a son; and since you are a son, God has made you also an heir" (Gal. 4:7). We experience a foretaste of our inheritance here and now. And so we **wait,** patiently and expectantly, **for his Son from heaven** (1 Thess. 1:10). We wait, too, with a healthy fear and trembling. F. F. Bruce reminds us, "To wait for him has ethical implications; those who wait are bound to live holy lives so as to be ready to meet him (see 5:6-8, 23)."[17]

Given the theological richness of this brief passage (1:8-10), it is not surprising that many scholars believe that verses 9b-10 are drawn from an early Christian hymn or from a portion of worship liturgy. It is closely packed with a great range of basic Christian doctrines. But Paul's intention in 1 Thessalonians is not primarily to provide grist for a theological mill; these truths are to be *lived*. John Stott notices the progression, "our gospel came to you"—"you welcomed the message"— **the Lord's message rang out from you** (1:5-8), and adds, "It is not enough to receive the gospel and pass it on; we must embody it in our common life of faith, love, joy, peace, righteousness and hope."[18]

3. DEFENSE OF THE MINISTRY 2:1-12

In this section, Paul and his colleagues continue to review their ministry among the Thessalonians, but now with a somewhat different emphasis. In 1:2-10, they briefly give God thanks for the way they were enabled to minister (1:5) and, at greater length, thanks for the way the Thessalonians were enabled to respond (1:6-10). But now, in 2:1-16, the missionaries describe more fully their own ministry (2:1-12) and then, more briefly, the Thessalonians' response (2:13-16).

There is also a defensive tone in their recollection here. Apparently, Paul feels it necessary to defend himself and his colleagues from charges as diverse as ineffectiveness, impurity, deceit, flattery, and greed (2:1-12). At this distance, we cannot be sure of the precise situation, but it is a reasonable conjecture that the synagogue authorities who had succeeded in getting Paul and company out of Thessalonica and then managed to do the same in Berea (see Acts 17:1-15), were trying to undermine the confidence of the new Christians by a campaign of defamation against the missionaries. We can imagine their vicious attacks: "They were just trying to exploit you." "As soon as things got rough, they deserted you." "Out of sight, out of mind; they have forgotten all about you."

Such accusations appear ridiculous to us, but we must remember that these were new Christians, without the historical perspective which enables us to arrive at a more balanced judgment. Indeed, we may know more about the Apostle Paul than they did! And there was another factor in their historical situation, well explained by Ernest Best: "It may seem almost laughable that Paul, who endured so much and appears to us so sincere, should seek so strenuously to defend the purity of his missionary activity, but the ancient world was full of wandering philosophers, prophets of new religions, magicians, 'divine men,' about whom secular writers warn as to their sincerity. . . . The *Didache*[19] warns about wandering Christian prophets who try to impose themselves on a community by settling down in it and living on it. . . ."[20]

Paul's primary concern was not his reputation as such, but the effect of these accusations on the new Christians. As we have already noticed in connection with 1 Thessalonians 1:6, the truth of the gospel is firmly bound up with the character and integrity of its messengers. This is especially true in the early stages.

With this background, let us look more carefully at the text to deduce what sorts of slanders Paul believes that the enemies of the gospel have been using to discourage the new Thessalonian Christians. The first part of the section is negative in tone as Paul denies certain accusations, and then it turns to a more positive description of how the missionaries have served. It is not easy to determine precisely where the change of tone occurs, partly because of some translation difficulty at verses 6 and 7, but a workable suggestion is as follows: negative defense (verses 1-6); positive defense (verses 7-12).

The opening words of the *negative* section (2:1-6) are emphatic in the Greek. **You know, brothers** (2:1) is literally, "You yourselves know." Whatever others may be saying, the Thessalonians know. Paul declares that his life has been an open book for the Thessalonians to read. He had already made that point in passing in 1:5, but now he makes it emphatic (2:1-2, 5, 9-11; see also 3:3-4; 4:2; 5:2).

Paul first refutes the claim that his and his colleagues' mission in Thessalonica was a failure. Perhaps the scoffers have been saying something like, "Nothing has really changed; it was all just a passing emotional experience, nothing permanent." But, in fact, the Thessalonians themselves are proof to the contrary. There is now a church in Thessalonica. There are **brothers** (along with their sisters; 2:1), members of the Christian family, already contributing to the advance of the gospel (1:7-8) and standing firm in spite of hardships (1:6). *They* are irrefutable evidence of the fruitfulness of Paul's brief stay in Thessalonica.

Further, in contrast to the traveling imposters exploiting the crowds in their own self-interest, Paul and his associates have persisted in their ministry in spite of frequent hardship and opposition. Most recently this occurred in Philippi, where they had suffered and been insulted (2:2; see New Revised Standard Version—"been shamefully mistreated"). The marks of their beating and chains (Acts 16:22-24, 33) still would have been visible when they came to Thessalonica. But they did not return to the security of their home church (Acts 13:13), nor even seek to maintain a low profile for a time. Rather, they courageously dared to tell the gospel in spite of strong opposition. This holy boldness testifies to their purity of intention and reveals a dedication to mission, possible only **with the help of our God** (1 Thess. 2:2). Their courage was God-given.

It is God's gospel (**his gospel** [2:2]), but He does not ordinarily send angelic messengers. He calls and prepares men and women to be His witnesses, near and far and in-between. Jesus promised that they would be equipped and empowered by the Holy Spirit (see John 20:21-22; Acts 1:8). Of course, the Holy Spirit is not mentioned in this immediate context, but God's help is expressed in another way. A more literal translation of **with the help of our God** (1 Thess. 2:2) is simply "*in* our God." And, in that protective embrace, Paul boldly declared **his** (God's) **gospel** (good news).

Because it is *God's* gospel, it is to be told in His way; there can be no tampering with the message, no unworthy motives, no dubious methods. First Thessalonians 2:3 implies that there have been accusations concerning the source of the missionaries' message (**error**); the integrity of their intentions (**impure motives**); and the honesty of their methods (**trick**). But Paul affirms their total trustworthiness, confident, as we have already noticed, of the Thessalonians' confirmation. J. B. Phillips helpfully rephrases Paul's denials, turning them into positive terms: "Our message to you is true, our motives are pure, our conduct is absolutely above board" *(The New Testament in Modern English)*. These high standards of content, motive, and method continue to serve as the marks of God's true spokespersons today.

Then, repudiating the false accusations with a strong **On the contrary** (2:4), Paul reinforces his claim to integrity in a positive affirmation. He has a sacred stewardship, having been **entrusted with the gospel** (2:4; see also 1 Corinthians 4:1-2; 9:17; Galatians 2:7; 1 Timothy 1:11; 2 Timothy 2:2; Titus 1:3), but only after having been **approved by God** (1 Thess. 2:4). The Greek word which lies behind **approved** is translated **tests** near the end of the verse. The same word is used again in 5:21: "Test everything," which is followed by, "Hold on to the good," and "Avoid every kind of evil" (5:21-22). The Greek word means to examine, scrutinize, evaluate to see whether genuine. It is possible to deceive men, of course, but not God, who **continually tests our hearts** (2:4; see also Psalm 7:9; 17:3; Jeremiah 11:20; 12:3; 17:10). And here, "heart" stands for the inner person in all its dimensions (see Acts 1:24; Romans 8:27; Revelation 2:23).

Paul knows that he is answerable to God (1 Cor. 4:4; 9:27), and this knowledge keeps him honest (2 Cor. 4:2). John Stott observes that a strong sense of accountability to God is "marvelously liberating" and adds, "To be accountable to him is to be delivered from the tyranny of human criticism."[21] Of course, there is room for a proper concern to please others (1 Cor. 9:19-23; 10:31-11:1; Rom. 15:1-3). Blessed is the servant of the Word who can keep these various considerations in proper balance.

Paul does claim, even under this scrutiny, **to please ... God,** although the New International Version weakens the language somewhat by adding the word **trying,** which is not in the Greek text (1 Thess. 2:4). Paul's claim may well give us pause. Did not Jesus teach us to pray regularly for the forgiveness of our trespasses (see Matthew 6:12)? Are we not all unworthy servants (see Luke 17:10)? Do we not fall short of complete obedience in word, thought, and deed?

It may help to notice that what God is testing is **our hearts** (1 Thess. 2:4), not our performance as such, at any stage of development. It has been said that God is easy to please, but hard to satisfy, as parents are *pleased* by their young child's first faltering steps, but will not long be *satisfied* unless there is continued progress. The need for growth is emphasized by the writer to the Hebrews in 6:1-6. Going on is the key, for falling back may lead to falling away.

Paul was **not trying to please men but God** (1 Thess. 2:4); therefore he **never used flattery,** as the Thessalonians could testify (**you know** [2:5]). Neither did he **put on a mask to cover up greed** (2:5), though only **God,**

who tests our hearts (2:4), could bear witness to *that*. **Greed,** the passion
for acquisition, is so prevalent in our contemporary consumer culture that
Christians in an affluent society may miss the severe criticism greed receives
in the New Testament. Jesus places it alongside "sexual immorality, theft,
murder, adultery . . . malice . . . lewdness" (Mark 7:21-22) as something
defiling (1 Cor. 5:10-11; 6:10) and, thus, excluded from His kingdom.

In Paul's words, **We were not looking for praise** (1 Thess. 2:6), the
translation **looking for** is probably too weak; "seeking" or even
"demanding" would make a better contrast with what follows. The next
phrase presents something of a translation problem. It may continue the
sentence, as in the New Revised Standard Version: "though we might
have made demands as apostles of Christ" (2:7a). Those demands
presumably would have included financial support (see 2:9). On the
other hand, the New International Version may be correct in beginning a
new sentence here: **As apostles of Christ we could have been a burden
to you, but we were gentle among you** (2:6-7a). In the long run, the two
translations produce much the same meaning—Paul and his colleagues
did not insist on being treated with great esteem, nor did they demand
financial support. In fact, Paul's style of ministry was just the opposite
(2 Cor. 4:5; 12:15).

Now begins a transition from a defensive description of the
missionaries' ministry to a more *positive* one (2:7-12). In the words **but
we were gentle** (2:7), the Greek word for **but** is a strong word, indicating
an emphatic contrast and signaling a change of direction. However, we
immediately face another translation problem—this time because of
differences among early Greek manuscripts. Some of them use the word
"gentle" and others use "babes." If we accept **we were [babes] among
you,** presumably the meaning would be that Paul and his fellow
evangelists became as children among children—they came down to the
level of the young Thessalonian Christians and perhaps, in effect, talked
baby talk to them rather than standing on their apostolic dignity and
lecturing in pretentious language. The manuscript evidence seems to
favor this reading, but the comparison seems rather out of harmony with
the context. **Gentle** fits into the train of thought more smoothly, and
leads naturally into the comparison of a mother with her children: **like a
mother caring for her little children** (2:7b).

The New International Version is close in its translation here, but the
New Revised Standard Version is a little more accurate: ". . . like a nurse
tenderly caring for her own children" (2:7b). "Her own children"
suggests even closer bonds of affection and concern than a nurse with

someone else's children. But either translation suggests loving concern, nurturing, providing, protecting. Elsewhere, Paul describes his converts as his children, usually from the perspective of a father (1 Thess. 2:11; 1 Cor. 4:14-16; 2 Cor. 12:14; but see Galatians 4:19).

We were delighted to share . . . our lives (1 Thess. 2:8) continues the theme of self-sacrificing love. The evangelists were not satisfied with performing only the basic duties of Christian ministry, such as proclaiming the gospel of God, but were prepared to share on the deepest level their lives as well. The word translated **lives** is the term older versions usually rendered as "souls." Ernest Best comments, "Paul gives not only what he has, the gospel, but what he is, himself. . . . The true missionary is not someone specialized in the delivery of the message but someone whose whole being, completely committed to a message which demands all, is communicated to his hearers. . . ."[22] The motive is love: **because you had become so dear to us** (2:8).

Now Paul presents further evidence that he and his associates were not seeking to exploit the Thessalonians, evidence they **surely . . . remember**—the missionaries' **toil and hardship** as they **worked night and day** to support themselves (2:9). **Toil** and **hardship** are almost synonyms; the first may point to the weariness and the second to the strenuous effort. **Night and day** does not mean twenty-four hours a day, but starting early and continuing late. Their motive was **not to be a burden** (2:9; see 2:7). So, far from seeking benefit for themselves, they worked hard and long to supply their own needs.

This is one aspect of the complex issue of ministerial support. The most extended treatment of Paul's policy on this question is 1 Corinthians 9:1-23. There he says he would go to any length to avoid conduct which would hinder the gospel (1 Cor. 9:12b). And certainly, appearing to be mercenary could raise the issue of "impure motives" (1 Thess. 2:3), and would alienate inquirers. Like Jesus, the evangelists came not to be served but to serve and even, in a sense, give their **lives as well** (2:8). There are other ways than literally dying to give one's life for a good purpose. F. F. Bruce reminds us that Jesus taught us ". . . not that lowly service will be rewarded by promotion to a position of greatness, but that, in his kingdom, lowly service *is* true greatness."[23] And in that pattern, the Apostle Paul was prepared to follow his Lord, (see 2 Corinthians 1:6; 4:5, 11-12; 12:15; Philippians 2:17; Colossians 1:24).

On the other hand, Paul argues in 1 Corinthians 9:3-12 that a missionary has a *right* to maintenance by the church, and Paul acknowledges receiving help from Philippi (Phil. 4:16). Perhaps he accepted gifts only after a church had become established. Second Corinthians 12:13-18 indicates that Paul's policy in these matters was not always understood, perhaps because of what appeared to be inconsistencies as he tried to adjust his financial practices to different situations.

It may be significant that the Greek verb forms behind **worked** and **preached** (1 Thess. 2:9) seem to indicate that the two activities were going on simultaneously. The book of Acts describes Paul preaching in a variety of settings: a synagogue (Acts 17:2; 18:4); the marketplace (17:17); a private house (18:7); a schoolroom (19:9); and an upstairs room (20:8). But the passage before us suggests another arena: the workplace (1 Thess. 2:9).

We can readily picture Paul working with Priscilla and Aquila in their tent-making shop (Acts 18:3), cutting, fitting, and sewing together pieces of leather. In a frequently quoted study, Ronald Hock observes, "It is difficult to imagine Paul *not* bringing up the subject of the gospel during the discussions with fellow workers, customers and others who entered the shop—given the relative quiet of a leather working shop, given the many hours Paul spent at work, given the utter commitment of Paul to gain converts for Christ, and given the sympathy that Paul showed in other ways for Cynic traditions."[24] "Gossiping the gospel" is an expression sometimes used to describe this method of spreading the faith. Obviously there is no place for badgering workmates, neighbors, or casual acquaintances, but well-placed, winsome words of testimony will bear fruit—*if* backed up by a life of personal integrity.

Because he has a clear conscience, Paul does not hesitate to appeal to both the Thessalonian Christians and to God as witnesses (1 Thess. 2:10) to testify to the **holy, righteous and blameless** quality of their lives among the new believers. It is difficult to distinguish the first two terms. Some think that **holy** refers to character, and **righteous** to behavior. Taking this a step further, the appeal to both divine and human witnesses may suggest defining **holy** primarily in relation to God and **righteous** primarily in relation to other people. **Blameless** claims that they were beyond reproach, perhaps by either God or man (1 Thess. 3:13; 5:23; Phil. 2:15; 3:6).

Appealing again to his readers' recollection, Paul declares that he **dealt with each of [them] as a father deals with his own children** (1 Thess. 2:11). The word **each** is emphatic and suggests one-on-one personal discipling (see Acts 20:20, where Paul describes his ministry as involving both going "house to house" and also teaching "publicly"). And Paul's spirit and manner were those of **a father . . . with his own**

children (1 Thess. 2:11). Paul unites the tenderness of **a mother** (2:7; see also Isaiah 66:13) with the strength of **a father** (1 Thess. 2:11; see also 1 Corinthians 4:14-17; Psalm 103:13). Ernest Best explains parental responsibility in that culture: "The mother cares for the child in its first few months but as it grows it has to be treated as a morally responsible being and advised how to live; this was the function of the father in the ancient world."[25]

The goal of the paternal training was to prepare young believers **to live lives worthy of God** (1 Thess. 2:12) or, literally, to "walk worthily of God." "Walk" was a common metaphor for pursuing a pattern of conduct; it is used some thirty-two times in the Pauline letters. It implies that the Christian life involves direction, progress, goal. Here the standard is **worthy of God,** that is, a life reflecting His character as revealed in Jesus Christ (see Philippians 1:27; Ephesians 4:1; Colossians 1:10). Paul's fatherly responsibility in this respect includes **encouraging, comforting and urging** his converts in that direction (1 Thess. 2:12). The three verbs overlap in meaning and are difficult to differentiate; together, they include ideas of exhorting, reassuring, and insisting. Obviously, different pastoral situations will require emphasizing sometimes the one, and sometimes the other.

But if the present aim is **lives worthy of God,** the ultimate goal is participation in God's **kingdom and glory** (2:12). The kingdom of God was, of course, a major element in the teaching of Jesus. The term occurs much less frequently in Paul's writings (but see Acts 20:25; 28:31). He does refer to its present reality (Rom. 14:17; 1 Cor. 4:20; Col. 1:13), but more often he puts it in the context of final things (2 Thess. 1:5; 1 Cor. 15:24, 50) and, as here, presents it as a motive for Christian conduct (1 Cor. 6:9-10; Gal. 5:21; Eph. 5:5). Its close association here with **glory** (1 Thess. 2:12) suggests that he refers to the future, full manifestation of the **kingdom** (see 2 Thessalonians 1:10-12; 2:14; Romans 5:2; 8:18; 2 Corinthians 4:17; Colossians 1:27). To this God **calls** (1 Thess. 2:12), and the verb form indicates that He *continues* to call. Paul describes God's call from different perspectives: a once-and-for-all call (Gal. 1:6); or a call heard in the past, but still continuing (1 Cor. 7:15, 17). Here Paul refers to the steady pressure of an ongoing call. One of the older commentators, C. J. Ellicott, notes the significance of this verb form: "The call is not simply a momentary act, but a *continual* beckoning upward until the privileges offered are actually attained."[26]

Before we leave this passage, we may note qualities of a missionary/evangelist/pastor set forth here: courage (2:2); integrity of content and method (2:3); sense of answerability to God (2:4); straightforwardness, honesty (2:5); unselfishness (2:6); a mother's gentleness (2:7); self-giving love (2:8); industriousness, unselfishness (2:9); integrity of character, purity of motives, openness in human relationships (2:10); paternal love, concern for the training and discipline of those for whom one is responsible (2:11); directing converts toward God and His will for their lives (2:12). Contemplating such standards, the Christian worker may need the reassurance of 5:24: "The one who calls you is faithful and he will do it."

4. FURTHER THANKS FOR THE THESSALONIANS' RESPONSE 2:13-16

This passage rounds out the first main section of the letter—Paul's account of his and his colleagues' ministry in connection with the founding of the Thessalonian church. Paul returns to the theme of thanksgiving to God for the good response to the gospel on the part of the Thessalonians. He is grateful, both for their initial receptivity and for their perseverance in spite of persecution. And Paul's mention of persecution prompts reflection on the destiny of the persecutors, especially in the case of his fellow Jews. This passage also prepares the way for the next section, in which Paul will acknowledge his anxiety as to how these new converts are faring under the continuing pressure (1 Thess. 3:3-5).

Therefore, these words of commendation are intended to motivate the Thessalonians to continued courageous loyalty to God. It is also possible that Paul may still be justifying his claim that the Thessalonian ministry has not been a failure (2:1; some interpreters make a connection even as far back as 1:6).

The progress of thought in this paragraph may be traced as follows:

a. The Thessalonians welcomed the Word (2:13)
b. The Thessalonians suffered persecution (2:14)
c. The Jews persecuted the church (2:15-16)
   i. The nature of the persecution (2:15-16a)
   ii. The result of the persecution (2:16b)

Paul begins by thanking God that, whatever suspicions and accusations others may have voiced concerning the missionary team, the Thessalonian converts received the Word of God (2:13); that is, they heard the message.

What is more, they accepted it; they *welcomed* it (2:13; 1:6; contrast 2 Thessalonians 2:10). And they welcomed the message for the best of reasons: Even though they heard it from men (**from us**), they recognized it as **the word of God,** and **not as the word of men** (1 Thess. 2:13). And, as **the word of God,** it has power; it works, it accomplishes that for which God has sent it (see Isaiah 55:10-11; Acts 20:32; Hebrews 4:12; James 1:21). And it is still at work in them.

But even the Word of God is ineffective without the right human response: **you who believe** (1 Thess. 2:13). This is reminiscent of other New Testament passages: Matthew 13:19-23; Hebrews 4:2; and note Jesus' warning, "He who has ears, let him hear" (Matt. 13:9). We should observe also that the form of the verb **believe** (1 Thess. 2:13) indicates an ongoing faith, not an isolated moment of commitment. God keeps on working in those who *continue* to exercise faith. The turnaround of conversion is just the beginning. The journey takes a lifetime.

The **for** at the beginning of 2:14 indicates that Paul is about to give evidence for his confidence that the Word of God is at work in the lives of the Thessalonian congregation. The proof is the way they are handling persecution. Some of the details in the rest of this paragraph are obscure, but Paul's main purpose seems clear. He encourages first by reminding them that they are not alone in experiencing persecution. It "goes with the territory," as shown by the examples of the Judean churches, Jesus himself, the prophets in earlier times, and now the apostles (note the reference to **us** in 2:15). Furthermore, their persecutors are setting themselves up for divine judgment by daring to oppose the purpose of God himself. They are certain to experience His **wrath** (2:16).

In this context of thanksgiving (2:13), Paul expresses one reason for his confidence that God is continuing to work in the lives of the Thessalonians. Verse 14 introduces an explanation and reason: **For you, brothers, became imitators. . . .** Paul does not mean *intentional* imitation, of course. But, as a matter of fact, they are having a similar experience, and they, too, are remaining faithful.

It is not obvious why Paul introduces the particular example of the **churches in Judea** (1 Thess. 2:14). Commentators suggest possible factors: these were the earliest churches and, thus, illustrate that persecution is part of the basic pattern of Christian life (3:4); Paul himself had once been among their persecutors (Acts 8:3); and the first opponents of the Thessalonian church had also been the local synagogue authorities (Acts 17:5-9). **Your own countrymen** (1 Thess. 2:14) may indicate that while the original trouble had been fomented by Jewish leaders, the participation by Gentile townspeople also continued (Acts 17:5-9).

In 1 Thessalonians 2:15-16, Paul describes the conduct of the Jews and its inevitable consequence. The language is unexpectedly severe, and appears to leave little room for qualification. Similar language is attributed to Jesus (Matt. 23:29-36; Luke 13:14). Also, Stephen's address, which Paul may have heard, contained strong denunciation (Acts 7:51-53). As Paul describes them here, the Jews have been consistent, at least: always **hostile** to both **God** and **men** (1 Thess. 2:15). The climactic act of rebellion was their role in the death of Jesus (Luke 20:9-19), but before that they had opposed the prophets, and after it they have hindered the ministry of the apostles (**us** [1 Thess. 2:15]).

Drove us out (2:15) seems clearly to refer to the episode reported in Acts 17:5-10; 13-14. But the book of Acts reports numerous other examples of Jewish opposition to Paul's evangelistic ministry: at Damascus (Acts 9:22-23); Pisidian Antioch (13:50); Iconium (14:2, 5); Lystra (14:14); Berea (17:13); and Corinth (18:12). And **so that they may be saved** (2:16) indicates the gravity of their offense: they were interfering with God's saving purpose.

The **all men** at the end of verse 15 is not to be taken literally, as if Paul were making his people out to be as hateful as some ancient authors did. The same pair of Greek words is used elsewhere for "people in general" or "all the people involved" and thus do not necessarily mean "the whole human race" (see 2 Corinthians 3:2; Philippians 4:5; Colossians 1:28).

The remainder of 1 Thessalonians 2:16 is extraordinarily difficult; some scholars place it among the most perplexing passages in the New Testament. The New International Version makes a new sentence here, beginning with **In this way;** however, in the original Greek this is the last clause of the preceding sentence, attached with the words "so as to," an expression which may indicate either a purpose or result to be named. Since the subject is **they,** referring to the Jewish persecutors, surely they do not *intend* to pile up sins and come under the judgment of God. Therefore, the more probable interpretation is that *as a result* of these activities, they heap up their sins to the limit. (For similar language see Genesis 15:16; Matthew 23:29-36, especially verses 32, 36.) The imagery may be that of a balance scale. As they keep adding more to one pan, at some point they will exceed God's counterbalancing patience, the scales will rotate, and they will experience divine judgment.

The meaning of the rest of the verse is uncertain; **has come** can mean "has arrived" or "has come near, is imminent." Commentators are divided. If Paul means to point to events which already have arrived, scholars mention three recent events which might be considered as warnings to Jewish leaders: (1) the famine of A.D. 46 (Acts 11:27-30); (2) Emperor Claudius's expulsion of Jews from Rome in A.D. 49 (Acts 18:2); (3) the massacre of Jews in the Temple precincts at Passover in A.D. 49, reported by Josephus, a first-century Jewish historian. Others think that **the wrath of God** which "has arrived" (1 Thess. 2:16) is a judicial blindness which has prevented Jews from recognizing Jesus as their Messiah, on the principle that refusing to use light leads to blindness (see John 9:30-41; Romans 1:24, 26, 28; compare the hardening of Pharaoh's heart—for example, Exodus 7:3).

If Paul intends something in the near future, on the other hand, he may be referring to the destruction of Jerusalem in A.D. 70. Does he know of Jesus' predictions (Mark 13:2, 30; see Luke 23:28)? Or does he simply mean that, given the logic of the situation, divine judgment is inevitable?

Many modern readers are uncomfortable with the apparently unqualified condemnation of Jews in 1 Thessalonians 2:13-16, especially verses 15-16. Some even describe it as "anti-Semitic." But it is appropriate to notice that, although Paul, in this context, is not careful to make the limitation explicit, he is not referring to *all* Jews, but only to those who were actively engaged in opposing the saving purpose of God. His fundamental attitude toward his own people is expressed in Romans 9:1-5 and 10:1 (see 1 Corinthians 9:20). And while a detailed interpretation of Romans 11 is puzzling, Paul's ultimate confidence shines through in the fact that God will include many Jews in His final saving acts, even, Paul says in a particularly enigmatic phrase, "all Israel" (Rom. 11:26).

ENDNOTES

[1]E. E. Ellis, "Coworkers, Paul and His," in Gerald F. Hawthorne and Ralph P. Martin, eds., *Dictionary of Paul and His Letters* (Downers Grove, Illinois: InterVarsity Press, 1993), p. 183.

[2]The Septuagint is the Greek version of the Old Testament, translated from Hebrew. It is often indicated by the Roman numerals LXX in accordance with the legend that it was translated by seventy scribes.

[3]William Barclay, *A New Testament Wordbook* (New York: Harper and Brothers, Publishers, n.d.), p. 35.

[4]Monotheism is the belief that there is only one God. The life and belief system of the Jewish people (Judaism) involves a covenant relationship with God, and though there are various branches of Judaism, the underlying theme among them is monotheism and a recognition of the Law, or Torah (the first five books of the Old Testament: Genesis, Exodus, Leviticus, Numbers, and Deuteronomy).

[5]Leon Morris, *The Epistles of Paul to the Thessalonians,* Tyndale New Testament Commentary (Grand Rapids, Michigan: Wm. B. Eerdmans Publishing Co., 1957), p. 33.

[6]Ernest Best, *A Commentary on the First and Second Epistles to Thessalonians,* Harper's New Testament Commentaries (New York: Harper and Row Publishers, 1972), p. 67.

[7]Best, p. 69.

[8]John Stott, *The Gospel and the End of Time* (Downers Grove, Illinois: InterVarsity Press, 1991), p. 31.

[9]The Gospels include the New Testament books of Matthew, Mark, Luke, and John. The Epistles are letters and include the New Testament books of Romans, 1 and 2 Corinthians, Galatians, Ephesians, Philippians, Colossians, 1 and 2 Thessalonians, 1 and 2 Timothy, Titus, Philemon, Hebrews, James, 1 and 2 Peter, and 1, 2, and 3 John.

[10]Best, p. 79.

[11]I. Howard Marshall, *1 and 2 Thessalonians,* New Century Bible Commentary (Grand Rapids, Michigan: Wm. B. Eerdmans Publishing Co., 1983), p. 115.

[12]Ibid., p. 59.

[13]The Incarnation was God's coming to us in the person of Jesus.

[14]Leon Morris, *The First and Second Epistles to the Thessalonians,* rev. ed., New International Commentary on the New Testament (Grand Rapids, Michigan: Wm. B. Eerdmans Publishing Co., 1991), p. 53.

[15]Stott, p. 39.

[16]William F. Ardnt and F. Wilbur Gingrich, *A Greek-English Dictionary of the New Testament* (Chicago: University of Chicago Press, 1957), p. 204.

[17]F. F. Bruce, *1 and 2 Thessalonians,* Word Biblical Commentary (Waco, Texas: Word Books, Publisher, 1982), p. 19.

[18]Stott, p. 44.

[19]The *Didache* is an early Christian writing, written about A.D. 112.

[20]Best, p. 99.

[21]Stott, p. 51.

[22]Best, pp. 102–3.

[23]Bruce, p. 31.

[24]Ronald F. Hock, *The Social Context of Paul's Ministry: Tent-making and Apostleship* (Philadelphia: Fortress Press, 1980), p. 41. The Cynics mentioned here were traveling teachers who called for personal integrity and for living in a manner independent of prevailing social expectations. Some scholars have recently proposed some parallels with the message and lifestyle of both Jesus and Paul. They proposed a simple lifestyle; one could carry all he needed in a knapsack (compare Matthew 10:9-10).

[25]Best, pp. 105–6.

[26]C. J. Ellicott, ed., *Bible Commentary: The New Testament,* vol. 9, Cambridge Bible for Schools and Colleges (London: Cassell and Co., Ltd., 1887), p. 90. Italics his.

2

PRESENT: TIMOTHY'S VISIT

1 Thessalonians 2:17–3:13

The preceding section was in large measure a defense of the ministry of Paul and his missionary colleagues when they were *present* among the Thessalonians at the church's founding. This section is, among other things, a defense of his *absence*. As previously mentioned, there is every likelihood that adversaries in Thessalonica had tried to undermine the new converts' confidence in the evangelists by personal attacks against them, such as "When things got tough, they took off and left you in the lurch," or "Now Paul has turned his attention to the Corinthians and forgotten all about you."

The main points of Paul's defense are clear: He tried to return, but his way was blocked (2:17-20); his continuing concern was so strong that he sent a valued colleague to visit them in his place (3:1-5); his anxiety has been relieved by Timothy's report (3:6-9); and he still longs to be among them again and prays to that end (3:10-12).

Paul bares his pastoral heart in this section, revealing to the Thessalonian Christians his loving concern for them, his joy over them, his pride in them. He worries about them, prays for them, rejoices over them. He is engaged in mission elsewhere, to be sure, but these Thessalonian spiritual children are never far from his mind. He opens his heart in this way, hoping to strengthen and encourage them in their Christian walk in the midst of adversity. He is ministering to them, but he wants them to know that they also minister to him; what happens in their lives touches him, even though he is miles away. The pastoral purpose which runs through this whole letter is especially evident in this section.

As mentioned in the introduction to the commentary, there were three principal ways in which Paul fulfilled his pastoral responsibilities to his congregations: (1) by his personal presence; (2) by sending a personal deputy in his absence; or (3) by letters. In this case, unable to do the first, he does the second, and then follows up with the third.

1. PAUL'S RETURN PREVENTED 2:17-20

The use of the term **brothers** frequently marks the introduction of a new section in this letter (1 Thess. 2:17; see, for example, 1:4; 2:1; 4:1, 13; 5:1, 4, 12, 25). The term stresses what Paul has in common with the Thessalonians: the same heavenly Father, the same Elder Brother, the same destiny (see Romans 8:29). It puts Paul on their level, in a sense, but also gives him a claim on them. And even though Paul knows that as their apostle he speaks with "the authority of the Lord Jesus" (4:2), he does not wish to be *authoritarian*.

Torn away (2:17) is a strong phrase. It can mean "orphaned," which would be a real twist of thought. He has already been "mother" (2:7) and "father" (2:11). Has he now become an "orphaned child"? Not likely, because the phrase can also be used for parents suddenly deprived of their children, which is obviously more appropriate here. But the idea of a sudden, violent and, therefore, traumatic separation is well conveyed by the use of **torn away.** It emphasizes that Paul's departure was not by his own choice (see Acts 17:5-10).

The separation is only in physical presence, **not in thought** (1 Thess. 2:17; the Greek uses "heart"), but still Paul feels **intense longing** for reunion, which leads him to make every effort to see them again. Verse 18 reiterates, and thus reinforces, the description of his desire which has impelled him to make repeated efforts, **again and again,** to get back to Thessalonica. John Wesley comments on verse 17: "In this verse we have a remarkable instance, not so much of the transient affections of holy grief, desire, or joy, as of that abiding tenderness, that loving temper, which is so apparent in all St. Paul's writings toward those he styles his children in the faith."[1]

How many efforts Paul made, how soon, and what obstacles there were all remain unspecified. Possible hindrances were illness (see Galatians 4:13; 2 Corinthians 12:7); the restrictions laid down by the governing authorities in Thessalonica (Acts 17:9); danger to Jason and other local Christians (Acts 17:9); and problems in Corinth requiring urgent attention (Acts 18:5-17). Whatever had blocked Paul's coming, evidently it did not prevent Timothy's making the journey, and presumably he had fully explained matters to the Thessalonians. Paul does not need to elaborate; he only affirms that behind it was the agency of Satan.

Satan—which means "Adversary"—is, of course, the foremost enemy of God. Therefore, he is also the enemy of God's people and, indeed, all humankind. He will be called "the tempter" in 1 Thessalonians 3:5, and will be identified as the powerful figure behind the Antichrist in 2 Thessalonians 2:9. Among his routine activities is obstructing the work of God's servants, and Paul sees his hand in whatever has prevented Paul's return to Thessalonica.

As the introductory **for** indicates (1 Thess. 2:19), Paul reaffirms his longing to see them (2:17) which had led to his repeated efforts to do so. The situation pictured here is the Final Judgment, as indicated by **in the presence of our Lord Jesus when he comes** (2:19). [Earlier editions of the New International Version include "Christ" in that phrase, while later editions and most other versions omit the title on the evidence from early manuscripts; the meaning is in no way changed.]

This is the first place in this first letter to the Thessalonians where the Greek word *parousia* (often translated **coming**) is used. In itself, the word means simply "presence," but it came to be widely used as a special term to designate an official royal visit with full honors. There are many examples of this use even in contemporary documents. In the early church, however, it came to be the accepted term for the return of Christ in power and glory. Why does Paul mention it here? Because only at the Second Coming will the books be opened and the genuineness of the Thessalonians' conversion and Paul's apostleship be publicly declared (see Philippians 2:16).

That will be a time for evaluating the work of Christ's servants (2 Cor. 5:10). Will Paul's efforts be proven "useless" (1 Thess. 3:5; see 2:1)? No! For his converts, standing true to the end in spite of persecution will vindicate Paul's apostleship (1 Cor. 9:2—Paul's converts are called "the seal of my apostleship" [1 Cor. 3:5-15]). Therefore, the Thessalonian Christians (along with others) are his **hope** (1 Thess. 2:19).

And on that occasion they will also be his joy (2:20), as a parent may say, "This child is my joy." I. Howard Marshall comments, "The reward of the missionaries is simply the work they have been able, by God's grace, to do and the feelings of joy and satisfaction which it produces. Such feelings are not wrong. . . . Some people find it hard to believe that God can want Christians to be happy, and thereby completely misunderstand his nature and purpose."[2]

In the phrase, **the crown in which we will glory** (2:19), **the crown** refers to the victory wreath placed on the heads of winning athletes (Phil. 4:1). **Glory,** sometimes translated "boasting" in the older versions, here means a legitimate pride, exultation over what God has done through His servant.

Paul then reinforces his point here by answering his own question, **What is our hope, our joy . . . ?** with another rhetorical question—**Is it not you?**—and finally with the emphatic declaration, **Indeed, you are our glory and joy** (1 Thess. 2:20). J. B. Phillips translates this, "Yes, you are indeed our pride and our joy!" *(The New Testament in Modern English).*

We may discern a double pastoral purpose in all these vigorously expressed protestations: If it should be the case that the Thessalonians have doubts—inspired by opponents' criticisms or occasioned by Paul's prolonged absence—he reassures them that his love for them remains constant; and he intends to strengthen their determination to remain steadfast in their faith, even in the midst of persecution.

2. TIMOTHY SENT 3:1-5

Prevented from returning to Thessalonica himself, Paul sends a trusted colleague to bolster the Thessalonians' courage in the midst of continuing opposition. **So** (1 Thess. 3:1) picks up the thought of 2:17-20, and **we could stand it no longer** (echoed in 3:5) expresses the intensity of Paul's concern for the Thessalonian converts. It was this concern which induced him to send Timothy, even though it would deprive Paul of Timothy's help in Athens. The exact cause of Paul's anxiety about the Thessalonians is not spelled out here, but reasonable conjectures would include (1) the sudden departure of the missionaries before there was time for thorough discipling, (2) the ongoing persecution the Thessalonians apparently were experiencing, and (3) fear that Paul's failure to return for further ministry would contribute to their discouragement.

Paul seems to have some discouragement to contend with himself. Leon Morris remarks that **left** is a strong word (3:1) and adds, "It expresses a sense of desolation which is reinforced by the emphatic *alone.*"[3] The abbreviated record here and in Acts leaves us with several questions, particularly (1) the whereabouts of Silas, and (2) why Paul was so reluctant to be alone in Athens. As for the first, a reasonable hypothesis is that Silas also has been sent back to Macedonia, perhaps to Berea or Philippi, on the same sort of errand that takes Timothy to Thessalonica. And, for the second, Acts 17 indicates plainly that Paul felt isolated and perhaps somewhat depressed in Athens (Acts 17:16-21), and this would only be intensified by the meager response to his ministry (17:32-34). Apparently he did not remain there long.

But whatever uncertainties there may be on some of the details, the point Paul is making to the Thessalonian Christians is clear: He wants them to understand the depth of his concern for them. Although it was a costly decision for himself, he was willing to send them his trusted, close and valuable colleague, a **brother and God's fellow worker** (1 Thess. 3:2).

As the margin in the New International Version indicates, the manuscript evidence for the text here is somewhat confusing, and there are theological questions as well. If **God's fellow worker** is accepted as the wording, does it mean fellow worker *with* God, or fellow worker (with Paul) *belonging to* God (see 1 Corinthians 3:9 for a similar problem)? Here, the task shared by Paul and Timothy (and perhaps God) is spreading the gospel of Christ. Whatever the uncertainties on some details of interpretation here, Paul is emphasizing the high caliber of the representative he has sent. He is making at least two points: His sending so valuable a colleague shows (1) the depth of his concern for them, and (2) that they should respond to Timothy's ministry as they would to Paul himself.

Timothy's mission among the Thessalonians was to strengthen and encourage them **so that no one would be unsettled by these trials** (1 Thess. 3:3). This sort of follow-up work is an essential aspect of pastoral ministry, part of the task of spreading **the gospel** of Christ (3:2), and here made urgent by the **trials** the Thessalonians were encountering.

Unpleasant as they were, these **trials** should not have taken the Thessalonians by surprise; they should have known that they **were destined for them** (3:3). The evangelists had **kept telling [them] that [they] would be persecuted** (3:4). This was part of basic Christian instruction in the early church: by Jesus (see Matthew 5:11-12, 44; 10:16-23; 24:9-14; John 15:18-16:4, 33); and by the apostles (see Acts 9:16; 14:22; 1 Peter 1:6; 3:13-17; 4:12-19; Revelation 2:10). Presumably, the Thessalonians were warned to expect opposition as a part of their preparation to endure it. If one knows beforehand that the road he is taking passes through some rough terrain, he will be expecting such hardships and, therefore, will be less likely to become discouraged or even to think he may have lost his way.

Destined implies that in some sense trials are appointed by God (1 Thess. 3:3). Difficulties are part of what it means to live as a Christian in this world, and, therefore, they are not to be taken as signs of God's displeasure. Rather, they are a sign that one belongs to the family of God (see Hebrews 12:7-13). Leon Morris describes hardship as "the means of teaching us many lessons," and "part of the process of living out the Christian life. . . . There is always some lesson to be learned from it. It is always part of our being shaped into what God would have us to be."[4] (He also recommends *The Problem of Pain* by C. S. Lewis as a helpful treatment of the topic.)

With **for this reason** (1 Thess. 3:5) Paul gets back to the main topic of the paragraph—Timothy's visit—and reiterates his intense concern, **when I could stand it no longer.** The focus of his concern is their **faith** (see 3:2, 5-7, 10) because that faith will also be the focal point of attack by **the tempter** (3:5). When the seed of the Word has been recently planted, Satan is sure to try to snatch it away to prevent its maturing and fruitfulness (see Mark 4:15), or to plant weeds in the same field to cause confusion (see Matthew 13:38-39).

In a context like this, **faith** embraces not only the content of belief, but also personal trust and commitment (faithfulness), leading to obedience. It is foundational in the Christian life (see Ephesians 2:8-10). Evidently Paul **was afraid** (1 Thess. 3:5) that somehow the new Thessalonian converts might have proved vulnerable. Apparently, Paul did not believe in the popular form of so-called "eternal security."

We might want to ask whether Paul's admission that he **was afraid** his efforts among the Thessalonians might prove to **have been useless** (3:5) is a confession of some weakness in his own faith. F. F. Bruce offers at least a partial explanation: "After being expelled from one place after another in Macedonia, Paul and the others might well have wondered if, in spite of their confident interpretation of the call of God (Acts 16:10), they had been divinely guided to that province after all."[5] Apparently, even apostles can have moments of unwarranted anxiety, even though they are not "unaware of [Satan's] schemes" (2 Cor. 2:11).

3. TIMOTHY'S REPORT 3:6-10

Now the mood changes as Paul conveys his jubilant response to Timothy's report upon his return to Paul, who is presumably now in Corinth (see Acts 18:5). The language is extremely warm and affectionate. **Just now** (1 Thess. 3:6) indicates that Paul is responding to their message through Timothy almost immediately. It serves to show both the depth of Paul's concern and intensity of his thankfulness.

Paul's gratitude focuses on two aspects of Timothy's good news about the Thessalonian converts: their faith and love. He had been concerned not only about their love among themselves, but also how the Thessalonian Christians felt toward the missionary team—their

memories of us (3:6). There could have been some bitterness because of the way the evangelists had suddenly departed, because of the persecution they had been enduring as a result of their accepting the gospel, or because of Paul's continued absence. But Timothy has assured Paul that the Thessalonian believers **have pleasant memories of** them and **long to see** them as eagerly as the missionaries **long to** return (3:6).

Timothy has also reassured Paul concerning the Thessalonians' faith; they were **standing firm in the Lord** (3:8). And this good news was a breath of life to Paul: **Now we really live** (3:8). In our colloquial language, it would have "killed" Paul if Timothy had reported that the Thessalonians had turned against him or that there had been a mass defection from the faith. And, apparently, he would not have welcomed any more bad news, for he was finding himself in the midst of **distress and persecution** (3:7). We have no way of knowing precisely what difficulties Paul was experiencing at that moment, but the missionary team had encountered opposition in one place after another in Macedonia and Achaia, including Corinth, where they now were (Acts 18:5-17). Among Paul's burdens had been his anxiety concerning the Thessalonians, and now *that,* at least, is relieved, and Paul can hardly contain the joy he feels **in the presence of . . . God** because of the report Timothy has brought (1 Thess. 3:9).

His first thought is thanksgiving, and he finds himself struggling for words: **How can we thank God enough . . . ?** (3:9). The anxiety concerning the Thessalonian converts which he has just acknowledged (3:1, 5) and confessed by implication (3:6, 8) has been expelled from his mind by Timothy's **good news** (3:6) and replaced by joyous adoration and profuse praise. And God's grace at work in the Thessalonians is the cause.

But that does not mean there is no further need for urgent intercession on their behalf. Rather, **night and day,** constantly, consistently, Paul prays fervently, earnestly on their behalf (3:10). He specifies two concerns: (1) to see them again, in person (literally, "to see your face"); and (2) to minister to them further, to supply what is lacking in their faith (3:10). He prays that this letter will makes its contribution to their progress in the faith, but it cannot accomplish as much as face-to-face ministry.

Charles Wanamaker reminds us how deep the need is for the discipling of young Christians in a situation like theirs: "Living in a culture shaped by the beliefs and values of the Christian condition, contemporary Christians are prone to forget or ignore the magnitude of the change in beliefs and values undergone by Paul's pagan converts in becoming Christians. This problem was compounded by the lack of any New Testament to document for them the Christian way of thinking and acting. Hence the primary burden rested upon Paul and his colleagues to 'Christianize' their pagan converts, and to a lesser degree their Jewish converts."[6]

The Thessalonian Christians still have needs. The Greek word translated here **supply** (3:10) has a range of meanings: mending, and so making ready for use (see Matthew 4:21); restoring (see Galatians 6:1); or preparing (see Hebrews 10:5). And the Greek word translated **what is lacking** (3:10) is also somewhat general; it is not clear whether it implies serious shortcomings, or refers to further teaching Paul would have given, had he been able to remain longer. Presumably the rest of this letter, which is serving in some sense as a substitute for his presence, gives some indication as to what the Thessalonians still needed. The first clue is the content of his immediate prayer on their behalf.

4. PRAYER FOR THE THESSALONIANS' GROWTH 3:11-13

The passage builds on "pray" in 1 Thessalonians 3:10, giving a sample of Paul's prayers for them. There are two main petitions, the second more complex than the first: (1) that he may be enabled to visit them soon (3:11); and (2) that their love may **increase,** producing growth in holiness, in preparation for the return of Christ (3:12-13). This prayer brings to an appropriate close both this immediate section (2:17–3:13) and the first main division of the letter (1:1–3:13). It also provides a transition to the second main division. The first request links clearly with the preceding section on Timothy's report, and the second request leads into the next section with its emphasis on holiness of life, Christian community, and the Second Coming.

Our God and Father himself and our Lord Jesus (3:11) will be echoed in 2 Thessalonians 2:16. In both cases, Paul seems to place God and the Lord Jesus on the same level in both Person and Work. The **our** attached to both names indicates that he is thinking of their relationship to believers: They are children of the heavenly Father and, therefore, called to love one another (1 Thess. 4:10); and they are servants (slaves) of Jesus who is their Lord and, therefore, called to a life of obedience (4:2).

The first petition, **clear the way for us to come to you,** expresses the genuineness and intensity of Paul's desire to minister among them in person once more (3:11). To do so would require removal of Satan's obstruction (2:18). As far as we know, it was several years before this desire was fulfilled (see Acts 19:21; 20:1).

The second petition (1 Thess. 3:12) is addressed to **the Lord,** and most scholars think that when Paul uses **Lord** without further definition, he usually means Christ. It may be initially surprising that Paul prays that their **love** might **increase** (3:12) immediately after mentioning his concern about their "faith" (3:10). The explanation is that by "faith" Paul meant more than their belief system; faith involves their total Christian life of trust in God. It is also true that Jesus taught that loving God and one's neighbor comprised the Law and the Prophets (see Matthew 22:37-40). And Paul has acknowledged that, in fact, the Thessalonian Christians do love (1 Thess. 1:3; see 4:9-12), but there is room for growth. The Greek words translated **increase** and **overflow** overlap in meaning and reinforce each other. The term rendered **increase** is frequently translated "abound," and this further strengthens the petition.

This growing love is to be directed first, to others in the Christian community—**each other**—and then across ethnic, social, and economic lines to **everyone else** (3:12). Apparently they have made a good start, at least among themselves (4:9-10), but they need to reach out to people around them (5:15; see Romans 12:17-21; 13:8-10; Galatians 5:14; 6:10). "Love your neighbor as yourself," Jesus commanded, but modern Christians (like others before them) sometimes have difficulty defining "neighbor"—even those of us who think we are "experts in the law" (see Luke 10:25, 29).

Paul then gives this petition a final nudge by adding **just as ours does for you** (1 Thess. 3:12). He has just been describing his loving concern for them, and earlier had spoken of their imitating him (1:6). Leon Morris observes, "It may be that under modern conditions the preacher is not wise to direct attention to himself. But it is still true that if a preacher's message is to carry conviction it must first be found in his own life."[7]

The New International Version begins a new sentence with the second petition in verse 13—**May he strengthen your hearts**—but in the Greek the sentence is continued as a *purpose* clause, and may be translated "in order to establish your hearts in holiness" and (though not explicitly in the language of purpose, there is the final goal) "that they may be found blameless at Christ's coming." This emphasizes the close connection between love and holiness, a connection made less obvious by the New International Version's separation of the two petitions. The intimate relation Wesley saw between love and holiness or Christian perfection is well known, as in his often quoted summary statement, "By perfection I mean the humble, gentle, patient love of God and our neighbour, ruling our tempers, words, and actions."[8]

As mentioned before, "hearts" stands for the whole inner person, thinking, feeling, willing; in a way, we can understand it as meaning "the real you." So the prayer moves from Christ's intensifying our love to strengthening our inner being for holiness of life in preparation for the return of Christ. The terms **blameless** and **holy** overlap, especially when the context is the final Judgment. But the first is obviously more negative—being found not deserving of condemnation before God (see 2 Corinthians 5:10); and the second, more positive—found in conformity with the character of Christ.

The language here suggests the context of the Judgment: **in the presence of our God and Father** (or, more literally, "before our God and Father") and **when our Lord Jesus comes** (1 Thess. 3:13). Characterizing **God** as our **Father** sends a twofold message: (1) as His children, we are under obligation to obey Him (see 2:12—"live lives worthy of God"); but (2) He is also the loving Father whose good news ("the gospel of God" [2:9]) is a message of " grace and peace" (1:1c). Characterizing Christ as our **Lord Jesus** reminds us (1) that as His servants (slaves) we are answerable to our Master, and yet (2) He is also "Jesus, who rescues us from the coming wrath" (1:10). I. Howard Marshall comments on the importance of the unity of Father and Son in judgment: "It means that we do not have to face any other God than the One who has revealed himself in Jesus. Equally it underlines the importance of Jesus Christ as the One authorized by the Father to bestow life and salvation."[9]

The final phrase here, **with all his holy ones** (3:13), is problematic. It emphasizes the awesomeness of the whole situation, but the actual membership of Jesus' entourage is not clear. The Greek word behind **holy ones** is commonly translated "saints," and is a standard New Testament term for believers. And believers are described as rising to meet the returning Christ in the air, both the "dead in Christ" and " we who are still alive" (4:16-17). But strictly speaking, only the dead in Christ come *with* Him; the living rise to *meet* Him. And the phrase before us refers to *all* **his holy ones** (3:13).

Many take this phrase to refer to an assembly of angels, seeing a probable allusion here to Zechariah 14:5 (see Psalm 89:7). And in the New Testament, angels accompany the Son of Man: Mark 8:38; Matthew 25:31; and especially 2 Thessalonians 1:7. Some interpreters have maintained that both angels and believers are intended, but that may be trying to have your cake and eat it too.

ENDNOTES

[1]John Wesley, *Explanatory Notes upon the New Testament* (London: Epworth Press, 1950), p. 757.

[2]I. Howard Marshall, *1 and 2 Thessalonians,* New Century Bible Commentary (Grand Rapids, Michigan: Wm. B. Eerdmans Publishing Co., 1983), p. 89.

[3]Leon Morris, *The Epistles of Paul to the Thessalonians,* Tyndale New Testament Commentary (Grand Rapids, Michigan: Wm. B. Eerdmans Publishing Co., 1956), p. 61.

[4]Leon Morris, *The First and Second Epistles to the Thessalonians,* rev. ed., New International Commentary on the New Testament (Grand Rapids, Michigan: Wm. B. Eerdmans Publishing Co., 1991), p. 97.

[5]F. F. Bruce, *1 and 2 Thessalonians,* Word Biblical Commentary (Waco, Texas: Word Books, Publisher, 1982), p. 67.

[6]Charles A. Wanamaker, *The Epistles to the Thessalonians,* New International Greek Testament Commentary (Grand Rapids, Michigan: Wm. B. Eerdmans Publishing Co., 1990), p. 139.

[7]Morris, *The First and Second Epistles to the Thessalonians,* p. 109.

[8]John Wesley, *A Plain Account of Christian Perfection* (London: Epworth Press, 1952), p. 112.

[9]Marshall, p. 102.

Part Two

THE THESSALONIAN CHURCH: PRESENT AND FUTURE

1 Thessalonians 4:1–5:26

The close of 1 Thessalonians 3 brings the first main division of the letter to a climactic conclusion in a torrent of prayer. The brief history of the young congregation has been reviewed, primarily in terms of the initial ministry of the apostolic team (1:1–2:16) and of Timothy's report from his recent follow-up visit (2:17–3:8). The tone has been consistently warm and loving, as Paul and his colleagues have sought to reassure the recent converts and to build up their faith in the face of continuing persecution.

The prayer at the end of 1 Thessalonians 3 makes the transition from the past (for which Paul can hardly "thank God enough" [3:9]) to present needs (further growth in faith [3:10]; love [3:12]; and holiness of life [3:13a]) with a view to the future, especially the return of the "Lord Jesus . . . with all his holy ones" (3:13b).

Paul has been reestablishing his personal and pastoral relationships with the congregation, especially in 3:6-10, and now he begins to deal more directly and explicitly with issues which require attention. Judging from the contents of the second half of the letter, Paul believes that they need further instruction concerning practical holiness, especially with respect to sexual morality and community living (4:1-12); clarification concerning the second coming of Christ as it pertains both to deceased believers and to the living (4:13–5:11); and guidance concerning congregational life and work (5:12-24).

3

PRESENT: PRACTICAL HOLINESS

1 Thessalonians 4:1-12

After a few sentences of reassurance to the Thessalonians (1 Thess. 4:1-2), Paul moves right into the call for practical holiness in life, especially in relation to sexual morality. The opening verses indicate that the Thessalonian converts have already been instructed concerning basic principles of Christian living and, in fact, are living to please God. And thus it might seem strange that they would require further admonition on what seems to us so basic a moral issue. But George Milligan explains that this is "a warning rendered necessary by the fact that in the heathen world *porneia* [sexual immorality] was so little thought of that abstinence from it, so far from being regarded as inevitable by the first Christian converts, was rather a thing to be learned."[1]

Paul and his colleagues are also concerned for the quality of the Thessalonians' community life more generally, both among themselves and in relation to their neighbors. And so again, the missionaries begin this new topic with words of reassurance (4:9-10a), and then caution that, for their own sake and for the sake of their influence upon outsiders, it is important they maintain lives of consistent respectability. The advice itself may seem to us rather commonplace, but we should take note of the range of motives the missionaries bring to bear.

1. INSTRUCTIONS GIVEN 4:1-2

In this part of the letter, Paul addresses problems he would have preferred to deal with face-to-face (see 3:10). He needs to be firm but tactful and, therefore, begins on an encouraging note, urging them to

61

continue as they have been doing, only to do so **more and more** (4:1), presumably more consistently, and perhaps also with a more informed understanding of the principles of Christian living.

Finally is a bit surprising in view of how much more Paul feels the need to say in this letter (4:1). In usage, the word frequently marks the transition to a new section, sometimes, but not always, the last (see Philippians 3:1). It perhaps would better be translated "And now . . ." or "Further. . . ."

Brothers (1 Thess. 4:1), as we have seen, frequently begins a new paragraph. But it also makes the point that this new section deals with life in the Christian community. These are family concerns. Until recently, many of these Thessalonian converts may have hardly known one another, but now they have the same heavenly Father and are learning to regard each other as brothers and sisters. They now have a whole new set of relationships, which grant privileges and bring responsibilities, and which create concerns for one another they never felt before.

And they have new priorities. The first is **how to live in order to please God** (4:1). The Greek text is stronger than the New International Version indicates. The New Revised Standard Version has "how you ought to live and to please God," and "ought" represents a word which is frequently translated *must*. It is often used in contexts where it expresses the will of God. And Paul is about to develop one aspect of God's will (4:3-8).

But first Paul will prepare the way with words of encouragement. He is not about to spring a great surprise, reveal some hidden cost of Christian discipleship which he had before concealed. They have been instructed, and basically they have been following orders. And "orders" is the proper term for it, because the word translated **instructions** (4:2) frequently occurs in military contexts and is equivalent to *commands*. Perhaps it is to emphasize this fact further that the text which might have read "*through* the Lord Jesus" is translated **by the authority of the Lord Jesus** (4:2).

At the same time, Paul's language is diplomatic—**ask** and **urge**—and he seeks to be encouraging: **as in fact you are living** (4:1). This seems to be typical of his approach. He recognizes what God is already doing in and among the Thessalonians (1:3, 7-8; 2:13-14; 4:9-10; 5:4-5).

Another and more subtle encouragement may be suggested by the phrase **in the Lord Jesus** (4:1). This has a twofold application here. On the one hand, it indicates the source of Paul's authority as a spokesman for Jesus Christ. Leon Morris neatly summarizes some implications of the phrase "in the Lord Jesus" in terms which any thoughtful pastor or teacher would aspire to make his or her own: "That is to say, he is not taking up any position of superiority, nor, on the other hand, is his attitude one of hesitant timidity. He speaks as one who has authority committed to him by the Lord. He speaks as one who has 'the mind of Christ' (1 Cor[inthians] 2:16b). He speaks to people who are, themselves, in Christ. He speaks of the conduct that befits people in Christ."[2]

It is important to recognize the second application of the phrase, "in the Lord Jesus," for it applies also to the Thessalonians. They, too, are *in* Christ Jesus, and thus they are experiencing newness of life—His life. But Paul wants them to **do this more and more,** in accordance with the instructions they have received from the Lord Jesus through His apostle (1 Thess. 4:1).

2. SEXUAL PURITY 4:3-8

Perhaps in response to problems among the Thessalonians reported by Timothy, Paul reinforces previous instructions (1 Thess. 4:1-2) concerning the maintenance of sexual purity in the Christian community. As mentioned above, in the Greco-Roman world, sexual looseness was common. Faithful monogamy, says F. F. Bruce, "was a strange notion in the pagan society to which the gospel was first brought; there various forms of extramarital sexual union were tolerated and some were even encouraged. A man might have a mistress *(hetaira)* who could provide him with intellectual companionship; the institution of slavery made it easy for him to have a concubine *(pallake),* while casual gratification was readily available from a harlot *(porne).* The function of his wife was to manage his household and be the mother of his legitimate children and heirs."[3]

Probably few of the Thessalonian converts enjoyed the social status or possessed the means fully to pursue such a lifestyle, but surely they would have been influenced by the patterns of thought and practice prevailing in their culture. Ernest Best appropriately quotes E. J. Bicknell: "A few months of Christianity could not be trusted to undo the habits of a lifetime."[4] Apparently some reinforcement was in order for the Thessalonian congregation. For the church is not to get its signals from the surrounding society. As Paul had just reminded the Thessalonians, he also told the Philippians, "But our citizenship is in heaven. And we eagerly await a Savior from there . . ." (Phil. 3:20; see 1 Thessalonians 3:13).

It is not certain whether there was in the congregation a particular instance of sexual immorality requiring attention. Some interpreters think Paul would not have praised the church so warmly had there been an unresolved case of that sort among them. In any case, the problem was so pervasive in that society that Paul felt obliged to touch on it frequently (for example, Romans 13:13; 1 Corinthians 5:1; 6:13; 7:2; Galatians 5:19; Ephesians 5:3; Colossians 3:5).

Here, Paul deals with it decisively by putting it in the context of God's will for Christian holiness (1 Thess. 4:3a); by describing in some detail appropriate sexual conduct (4:3b-6a); and by giving three reasons for living the life of practical holiness (4:6b-8).

Paul begins with what we may call "the bottom line": **It is God's will that you should be sanctified** (4:3). It should be noted that earlier editions of the New International Version have **holy** here, where more recent editions use **sanctified.** Probably the change was made, properly, to distinguish between the form of the word used in 3:13, which, generally speaking, refers to holiness as a finished product and the form used here, which indicates the process of sanctification.

Obviously, Paul's "bottom line" connects directly with **how to live in order to please God** (4:1). It also rests squarely on a basic Old Testament theme: God is holy and, therefore, His people must be holy (see Leviticus 11:44-45; 19:2; 20:7, where the following context names various sexual sins; 1 Peter 1:16). Paul and his colleagues rejected the works-righteousness of legalistic Judaism, but they emphatically maintained the high ethical standards of the Old Testament.[5] This is an emphasis which is acutely needed today, says John Stott: "There is an urgent need for us, as pluralism and relativism spread world-wide, to follow Paul's example and give people plain, practical, ethical teaching."[6]

We have already indicated that when Paul prayed in 3:13 for the Thessalonian Christians to become "blameless in holiness" (the New International Version reads "blameless and holy"), the term he used means holiness as a resultant state, the completed process. This was appropriate in the context of the final Judgment. But here a literal translation would be, "This is God's will, your sanctification." And it is generally agreed among scholars that the Greek term used here refers to the *process* of sanctification, the ongoing work of God in the lives of believers. This is a widely used word in the New Testament (for example, 1 Thessalonians 4:3, 7; 2 Thessalonians 2:13; Romans 6:19, 22; 1 Corinthians 1:30; 1 Timothy 2:15; Hebrews 12:14; 1 Peter 1:2). It will be appropriate to say more about various aspects of sanctification in connection with 1 Thessalonians 5:23.

Here Paul goes on to express what Christian holiness requires with respect to sexual conduct. Ernest Best makes the thought-provoking comment, "Sanctification is not something for worship alone but for every act of life."[7] Among many other things, sanctification also requires **that you should avoid sexual immorality** (4:3). That is to say, this total avoidance (the Greek word here for **avoid** is a strong one) is one aspect of the holiness God commands and enables. As F. F. Bruce puts it, "chastity is not the whole of sanctification, but it is an important element in it, and one which had to be specially stressed in the Greco-Roman world of that day."[8] (It would be stating the obvious to add that, given the trends in modern North American society, it needs to be stressed once more.) It should be noted that the Greek word translated here **sexual immorality** is a broad term for sexual misconduct; it includes adultery, fornication, prostitution, and deviant sexual behavior.

The next verses (4:4-6a) describe more fully the sexual practices which are (4:4) and are not (4:5-6a) compatible with holy living. First, verse 4 is preventative in nature; it seems to be intended to indicate the proper course to take in order to abstain from sexual immorality. But, as the marginal reading indicates, the precise meaning of the clause is particularly difficult to determine. The alternatives are (1) as in the main text, **that each of you should learn to control his own body;** or (2) as in the margin, "live with his own wife." The debate circles around the meaning of the Greek word used here for body—*skeuos,* which means "vessel, tool, utensil," and is elsewhere used for household utensils and containers (for example, Luke 8:16; Revelation 2:27). Here the term is obviously being used as a figure of speech or point of comparison; the question is whether it stands for "body" or for "wife."

The application here puzzled even the early church fathers, and it is not likely that we can resolve the issue with certainty at this distance of time and culture. We will note the main arguments, and then move on.

First, consider that *skeuos* here means "body." It may be significant that this is the view of the majority of early Greek commentators, who obviously were much closer to the situation than we. Many see a rough parallel in 2 Corinthians 4:7—"We have this treasure in jars of clay"— and perhaps also in Acts 9:15 and Romans 9:21. There is a closer parallel in the Greek Old Testament at 1 Samuel 21:5 (see the margin in the margin of the New International Version), where the context indicates that sexual intercourse is the issue. But against this interpretation is the fact that the word translated **control** (1 Thess. 4:4) basically means "to acquire or possess," and we can hardly be advised to *acquire* a body. However, there is some evidence that in the common Greek of the New Testament period, the word had come to mean "possess" or even "to gain mastery over," which obviously would be appropriate with "body" in this context. There is also the advantage that, understood this way, the instruction applies to both men and women, married and single.

Second, consider that *skeuos* here means "wife." There may be a rough parallel in 1 Peter 3:7, where in the King James Version the wife is called "the weaker vessel," although the parallel is imperfect because the implication there is that the husband is also a vessel, only a stronger one. It does fit better with a verb meaning "acquire"—"how to take a wife for himself" (see New Revised Standard Version). However, this could easily be understood as a low view of marriage as primarily an antidote for sexual immorality. Sometimes reference is made to 1 Corinthians 7:2 in support of this view. But, as F. F. Bruce points out, in that passage sexual immorality is avoided, not by the man's having a wife, but by each man having his own wife and every woman her own husband: "The relationship is mutual and neither is the [vessel] of the other, both being persons in their own right."[9]

In any case, the main thrust of the passage is clear: Paul calls upon the Thessalonian Christians to abstain from all sorts of sexual misconduct by doing what is right, whether by self-control or by restricting sexual activity to the marriage partner. This is the way in which Christians can fulfill the apostle's call elsewhere to "honor God with your body" (1 Cor. 6:20; note preceding context there).

Paul next amplifies God's requirement concerning marriage and does so, first, in positive terms: **in a way that is holy and honorable** (1 Thess. 4:4). The literal translation is "in sanctification and honor." "Sanctification" (same term as **sanctified** in 4:3a) indicates that sexual expression, in and of itself, is not "dirty," but rather clean and pure. As I. Howard Marshall observes, "Holiness extends to the physical aspects of life; it does not exclude sexual activity . . . but controls its character."[10] Elsewhere, Paul does commend celibacy, but only for those who have been so gifted by God (1 Cor. 7:7).

But sexuality, though God's good gift, may be abused. Therefore, Paul next indicates how it can be debased: **in passionate lust like the heathen, who do not know God** (1 Thess. 4:5). **Heathen** here is the word usually translated *Gentiles,* but in this context the issue is not racial status as such, but religious understanding, as the next clause indicates. Paul expects that those who know God will act on the principle of love. "Christians must behave in a completely different manner because we do know God, because he is a holy God, and because we want to please him" (John Stott).[11]

But some who do not know God will act in **passionate lust** (4:5)—that is, with a selfish possessiveness which uses the partner for one's own gratification. The kind of persons Paul has in mind are those he will describe more fully in Romans 1:18-32. They do not know God because they have rejected His revelation of himself which is available to all humankind through nature, reason and conscience (nature is emphasized here; Rom. 1:20). The consequence is that they turn to idolatry and to "every kind of wickedness" (1:29), including sexual perversion (1:26-27).

That was the world Paul saw around him. And the more things change, the more they remain the same. Today's idols may not be "images made to look like mortal man" (Rom. 1:23), but wealth, power, reputation, etc. Their sins may be more sophisticated, their self-centeredness more subtle. But, having "exchanged the truth of God for a lie" (Rom. 1:25), they live for themselves, prepared to use others for their own ends, including sexual exploitation.

And in 1 Thessalonians another aspect of sexual immorality is mentioned: **No one should wrong his brother or take advantage of him** (1 Thess. 4:6a). Not only does it exploit the sexual partner; the transgressor also "wrongs" others. The original connotation of the word was crossing a boundary, thus trespassing on another's domain. And those injured include, of course, the mates of both offending parties and, indeed, the whole Christian family in that place—all of them "brothers" (and sisters), entitled to love and loyalty. And the damage may reach even farther (4:12a).

Implicit motives for following these instructions have been woven through the text, but the authors begin to introduce three direct appeals (4:6b). In the Greek text there is a "because" in the middle of verse 6 (which the New International Version omits), and then three reasons for pursuing the holiness of life in sexual practices. They follow in quick succession: Disobedience brings divine judgment (4:6b); sexual purity is one aspect of God's call (4:7); and rejecting this teaching constitutes a rejection of God (4:8). The case can be made very concisely because the missionaries have earlier **told** and **warned** the Thessalonians (4:6b; also 4:1-2, 11).

The first argument is very straightforward: **The Lord will punish men for all such sins . . .** (4:6b). Actually the New Revised Standard Version is closer to the original language: "Because the Lord is an avenger in all these things." The translators of the New International Version may have wished to avoid using "avenger," because the word may have harsh, sub-Christian connotations to our ears. But, of course, as applied to God or Christ (probably the latter, as is the usual meaning of "Lord" by itself in the Pauline writings; note the shift to **God** as subject in the next sentence [4:7; see 2 Thessalonians 1:8]), the term does not connote vindictive or capricious judgment, but rather giving just due, or treating as deserved. The Greek verb with the same root is used in Luke 18:3, where both the New International Version and the New Revised Standard Version correctly translate, "Grant me justice." (We may note that 1 Corinthians 11:30 indicates Paul's belief that the punishment *may* not wait until the final Judgment.)

After this warning, the second argument is stated positively: **For God did not call us to be impure, but to live a holy life** (1 Thess. 4:7). Literally, the last clause is "in sanctification" (as process). In one sense, the whole of the Christian life rests upon the divine call. This is especially clear in this letter (4:7; 2:12; 5:24), but the theme is found in other Pauline writings, too (2 Thess. 2:14; Rom. 1:7; 1 Cor. 1:2; Eph. 4:4; Col. 3:15; 2 Tim. 1:9; and see 1 Peter 1:15). And the right use of sex is one aspect of the holy life to which God calls us.

The third argument draws a conclusion: **Therefore, he who rejects this instruction does not reject man but God, who gives you his Holy Spirit** (1 Thess. 4:8). Actually, the word **instruction** is not present in the Greek text. Thus, we have "the one who rejects," and the object of his or her rejection is not a set of rules nor a human agent, but God himself. And God is the Giver of the Holy Spirit. Paul does not develop the point here, but in 1 Corinthians 6:18-20 he spells out more fully the significance of the Holy Spirit's presence in the Christian's life in relation to sexual immorality. Such conduct is totally out of place in the Christian community and constitutes defiance of God himself. However morally bankrupt the society may be in which one seeks to live an authentic Christian life, he or she need not conform to the prevailing pattern. The God who *calls* to sanctification also *enables* holy living through the gift of the Holy Spirit (1 Cor. 6:13-20).

3. CHRISTIAN COMMUNITY 4:9-12

The new paragraph clearly continues to be concerned with the quality of life in the new Christian community, but it is difficult to discern precisely what problem is being addressed for the Thessalonians. The first part seems perfectly general, and then in verse 10 there is a subtle shift to something more definite, but still difficult to define. The Apostle Paul begins by asking the Thessalonians to continue to exhibit mutual love, in fact, to **do so more and more** (1 Thess. 4:10b), and then calls for living quiet and self-sufficient lives, as if *that* were somehow a particular application of his call for living in love.

In this context it is appropriate to point out two features which outsiders noticed concerning the early church: (1) their self-control with respect to sexual conduct and to their use of wine; and (2) their love for one another. An early critic, apparently observing in the same congregation rich and poor, sometimes even slaves and their masters, meant to ridicule Christians when he said, "Their Master makes them think they are all brothers."

It is significant that the word behind **brotherly love** here is not the familiar *agape,* but rather *philadelphia* (4:9; see Romans 12:10; Hebrews 13:1; 1 Peter 1:22; 2 Peter 1:7). In secular usage it was a term for affection between and among biological brothers and sisters. Only among Christians was it used to express the reality of being members of the family of God. Charles Wanamaker remarks that, unlike the common Greek word for "brothers," this "constitutes an example of ancient inclusive language, since it was applied to both brotherly and sisterly love."[12] But, if this is to be more than a figure of speech, there are practical implications, and Paul is getting ready to point to the application which the Thessalonian Christians needed to make.

Paul begins tactfully by saying that on this topic **we do not need to write to you** (1 Thess. 4:9). Of course, he *does* write about it, but he has begun on an encouraging note. The source of their mutual love is **God** (**taught by God** [4:9]; see Isaiah 54:13; John 6:45; 13:34). Its God-given character is demonstrated by the fact that it reaches out beyond the more immediate friends and acquaintances to **all the brothers** [and sisters] **throughout Macedonia** (1 Thess. 4:10). Some interpreters see here evidence that Paul made an effort to establish networking among the churches he had founded in a given area (see 1 Corinthians 16:1, 19; 2 Corinthians 1:1; Galatians 1:2). This would make for a mutual support system, especially needed when they were so much in the minority and often objects of suspicion, or even targets for persecution. Among practical benefits would be hospitality for traveling bothers and sisters (as mentioned in connection with 1:7-8; see 3 John 5-8).

A critic of early Christianity meant to underscore their naiveté when he said, "They love even before they know each other." The explanation is their common bond in Christ, of course, as many even today have experienced when, for example, meeting fellow Christians in a mission situation where they do not know the language or understand the culture. To the Thessalonian converts, Paul says, "You *are* doing it." He can only urge them **to do so more and more** (1 Thess. 4:10). There is always room for growth in Christian graces, perhaps especially in this, the distinctive mark of Jesus' followers (John 13:34-35).

Leon Morris cites a searching word on this topic from James Denney, who reflects that many Christians, "if they looked into the matter, might find that few of their strongest affections were determined by the common faith. Is not love a strong and peculiar word to describe the feeling you cherish toward some members of the Church, brethren to you in Christ Jesus? Yet love to the brethren is the very token of our right to a place in the Church for ourselves." "These words," adds Morris, "are not yet out of date."[13]

However, it should be acknowledged that the Greek sentence structure here is somewhat ambiguous and the doing **so more and more** (1 Thess. 4:10) may be connected with the call for responsible living which follows. In any case, a more or less literal translation here would be, "We exhort you to strive to be quiet, mind your own affairs, and work with your hands," then a parenthetical "as we instructed you," and finally, two reasons: "that you may live appropriately before outsiders" and "that you will not be dependent on anyone."

It is impossible to reconstruct with certainty the situation which required such instructions. "Warn those who are idle" (5:14) may provide a clue, and many think that the stronger and more detailed instructions in 2 Thessalonians 3:6-15 confirm that some among the Thessalonians had given up regular work and had become idle busybodies, perhaps in the belief that the return of Christ was immediately at hand. To be sure, no connection with the expectation of the Second Coming is clearly stated here, but that *is* the topic of the next paragraph.

Another possible factor in the situation is the Greek attitude toward manual labor; they regarded it as degrading, suitable only for slaves. On the other hand, manual labor was regarded as dignified in Judaism.[14] In fact, a common saying had it that a father who did not teach his son a trade was teaching him to be a thief. Even rabbis were expected to learn a practical trade; Paul, for all his "academic" training, was also a tent maker. Certainly his example and instruction among the Thessalonians had been in this Jewish tradition (2:7, 9; see 2 Thess. 3:7-10).

The precise thrust of **make it your ambition to lead a quiet life** (1 Thess. 4:11) is not obvious. There is even something self-contradictory in the language used here, as some have indicated by translating, "Make it your ambition to have no ambition," or "Strive to be quiet." It is possible that it was intended as advice to keep a low profile in public so as to avoid inviting further unwelcome attention from city authorities (see Acts 17:8-9). Other interpreters take their cue from the phrase which immediately follows and understand being quiet to mean, in part, at least, the opposite of being a busybody.

Apparently the latter was a persistent problem (2 Thess. 3:11), and, of course, meddling *can* sow dissension in a congregation, even when no malice is intended. It is possible that the very sense of being a family in Christ which Paul has applauded was being taken too far by some who, perhaps with good intentions, felt entitled to invade the privacy of others. F. F. Bruce observes, "There is a great deal of difference between the Christian duty of putting the interests of others before one's own (Phil[ippians] 2:4) and the busybody's compulsive itch to put other people right."[15]

The sense of being family may also have contributed to the problem of idleness, if some felt that being members of the family entitled them to be supported. But Paul calls for a responsible work ethic. That was the model he had set before them (1 Thess. 2:9; 2 Thess. 3:7-10). Later, in a letter to the Ephesian church he would write, "He who has been stealing must steal no longer, but must work, doing something useful with his own hands, that he may have something to share with those in need" (Eph. 4:28). Again, working with one's hands is mentioned, but the emphasis is not on manual labor as such. Rather, the issue is being industrious rather than idle.

In general, they are to be Christian in their work habits. Noting the proportion of their time most workpeople spend on the job, Leon Morris cites another provocative comment by James Denney: "If we cannot be holy at our work, it is not worth taking any trouble to be holy at other times."[16] This is an important aspect of Christian witness (1 Thess. 4:12a). Two reasons are given for these admonitions: (1) so as to create a favorable impression among outsiders; and (2) so that they may provide for themselves, and thus be independent.

In relation to others, they are to live quietly, mind their own affairs, and work conscientiously so as to command the respect of non-Christians and thus strengthen their witness in the community (see Matthew 5:16; 1 Corinthians 10:32; Colossians 4:5; 1 Timothy 3:7; 1 Peter 2:12; Acts 2:47). F. F. Bruce comments, "Non-Christians must be given no pretext for thinking that Christians were unprofitable members of society. The church could not discharge its ministry of witness and reconciliation in the world unless its members adorned the gospel with their lives as well as proclaiming it with their lips."[17]

Furthermore, responsible living and working would mean that they would not have to be dependent upon others. Christians should not be seen as parasites. Of course, persons in genuine need should receive help (Rom. 12:8; 15:26-27; Gal. 2:10; 6:10).

Before leaving this section, as a stimulus to evaluating our own theological commitment and practical performance, and perhaps that of the fellowship of which we are a part, it may be useful to notice the variety of motives, stated and implied, to which Paul appeals in these verses. Some of the more obvious, enumerated in simple staccato fashion, are the following: they are brothers (1 Thess. 4:1); they have a good record (4:1); they have been instructed "in the Lord Jesus" and "by the authority of the Lord Jesus" (4:1-2); holy living is God's will (4:3); they should be different from nonbelievers (4:5); they should be concerned for their brothers/sisters (4:6a); the threat of the Lord's punishment (4:6b); the implications of God's call (4:7); disobedience is rejection of God (4:8a); God gives His Spirit to enable obedience (4:8b); they have been taught by God (4:9); they have been doing so and (implied) they should be consistent (4:10); their apostle is urging them (4:10b); Christian lifestyle will gain the respect of outsiders (4:12); and thus they will have the satisfaction of providing for themselves (4:12b).

Finally, if the question is asked whether the Thessalonians responded well to these urgings by their missionaries, 2 Corinthians 8:1-5 suggests that they did.

ENDNOTES

[1]George Milligan, *St. Paul's Epistles to the Thessalonians* (Grand Rapids, Michigan: Wm. B. Eerdmans Publishing Co., 1952), p. 48.

[2]Leon Morris, *The First and Second Epistles to the Thessalonians,* rev. ed., New International Commentary on the New Testament (Grand Rapids, Michigan: Wm. B. Eerdmans Publishing Co., 1991), p. 114.

[3]F. F. Bruce, *1 and 2 Thessalonians,* Word Biblical Commentary (Waco, Texas: Word Books, Publisher, 1982), p. 82.

[4]Ernest Best, *A Commentary on the First and Second Epistles to the Thessalonians,* Harper's New Testament Commentaries (New York: Harper and Row Publishers, 1972), p. 160.

[5]Morris, *The First and Second Epistles to the Thessalonians,* p. 155.

[6]John Stott, *The Gospel and the End of Time* (Downers Grove, Illinois: InterVarsity Press, 1991), p. 77.

[7]Best, p. 165.

[8]Bruce, p. 82.

[9]Ibid.

[10]I. Howard Marshall, *1 and 2 Thessalonians,* New Century Bible Commentary (Grand Rapids, Michigan: Wm. B. Eerdmans Publishing. Co., 1983), p. 109.

[11]Stott, p. 86.

[12]Charles A. Wanamaker, *The Epistles to the Thessalonians,* New International Greek Testament Commentary (Grand Rapids, Michigan: Wm. B. Eerdmans Publishing Co., 1990), p. 160.

[13]Leon Morris, *The Epistles of Paul to the Thessalonians,* Tyndale New Testament Commentary (Grand Rapids, Michigan: Wm. B. Eerdmans Publishing Co., 1957), p. 80.

[14]See endnote 5 above.

[15]Bruce, p. 92.

[16]Morris, *The First and Second Epistles to the Thessalonians,* p. 132n.

[17]Bruce, p. 93.

4

FUTURE: RETURN OF CHRIST

1 Thessalonians 4:13–5:11

The return of Christ has been mentioned at key points in earlier parts of this letter: The Thessalonian Christians wait for God's Son from heaven (1 Thess. 1:10); when He comes, they will be their apostle's pride and joy (2:19); their holiness of life will be tested in the presence of God when the Lord Jesus comes with all His holy ones (3:13). On that day, there will be wrath (1:10) and glory (2:19). Therefore, the prospect of Christ's return is both fearful and wonderful; it generates both apprehension and anticipation.

The Greek word the New Testament frequently uses for this event is *parousia,* a term which has passed into English usage, particularly among theologians and biblical scholars. The word itself basically means "presence," but William Barclay explains its special use for "the arrival of an emperor, a king, a governor or famous person into a town or province," and then he spells out some of the practical implications: "For such a visit preparations had to be made. Taxes are imposed, for instance, to present the king with a golden crown. . . . Always the coming of the king demands that all things must be ready."[1] The appropriateness of applying such a concept to the return of Christ is obvious—only it is raised to the nth degree! To participate in the celebration for the parousia of the King of Kings, even as one among multitudes in the welcoming crowd, would be an exhilarating experience, and just the beginning of the eternal celebration in His presence!

This glorious hope provides the background for the anxious questions asked by the Thessalonian Christians, particularly those who recently lost loved ones. Apparently these Christians fear that believers who have died will miss out on the joy of the Parousia. Paul eases their concern on that point by assuring them that Christians who have died before Christ's return will indeed participate fully in the celebration at His advent and, in fact, will even enjoy a certain privileged position ("first" [4:16]).

It seems that some others in the Thessalonian congregation have a different problem: As they think about Christ's return, they are apprehensive. They know "very well" that Jesus' second coming will be sudden, unexpected, and inescapable (5:1-3). And they probably share the general expectation among first-century Christians that it will be very soon. They are uneasy. Will they be found acceptable? Reassuring them in their anxiety, Paul masterfully interweaves encouragement (5:4-5, 9-10) and exhortation (5:6-8). They need to be alert and self-controlled (5:6), but the source of their confidence is God's gracious provision of salvation through Christ.

It is not entirely surprising that such questions could arise among these relatively recent Christians in Thessalonica. We cannot doubt that Paul had given them *some* instruction concerning the Resurrection; it was fundamental in the gospel he preached (see 1 Corinthians 15:1-3). But his time among them was too brief to permit following up on all its implications for those who belong to Christ. The missionaries were compelled to leave abruptly and unexpectedly, before they could have completed all the teaching they wanted to do (see Acts 17:5-10). Apparently, this is one topic on which the Thessalonians' understanding of the faith is still lacking (1 Thess. 3:10).

As their unanswered questions indicate, the Thessalonians need more information, more theological data. But that is not all. As Ernest Best perceives, "Paul writes as a pastor rather than as a theologian, but all good pastoral counseling is based on, and contains, theological teaching and not mere consolation."[2] Here, the additional theological facts Paul provides are limited to those directly connected with their particular questions. This passage says nothing specific about such issues as the situation of those not in Christ at the Second Coming or about the intermediate state (the period between the believer's death and resurrection). Paul's purpose is to reassure his beloved Thessalonian converts on the issues which were giving them concern *at that moment*.

1. REASSURANCE CONCERNING DECEASED CHRISTIANS 4:13-18

Only a short time can have elapsed since Paul was among the Thessalonian Christians, but it appears that some of their number have died already. Paul had proclaimed there the return of Christ (5:1-2), as he did elsewhere. But, somehow, they fear that deceased believers might not fully participate in the glory of Christ's coming. Perhaps they think that these deceased believers will not rise from the dead until a general resurrection at a later stage in the series of end-time events, *after* Christ's glorious appearing. In any case, whatever their specific (mis)understanding, the apparent result is that some of the Thessalonian converts are grieving excessively over the loss of loved ones, at least, for the wrong reasons (4:13).

Questions concerning the status of deceased Christians are not likely to occur in the course of evangelistic preaching, nor even in the earliest stages of discipling. But now the issue has arisen and presumably Timothy has reported it to Paul. In 4:13-18, Paul addresses the question and, on the basis of revelation (**According to the Lord's own word;** 4:15), sheds further light on final events in such a way as to provide a reassuring answer with which they may comfort one another (4:18).

We do not want you to be ignorant about those who fall asleep (4:13). These opening words appear to be a sort of formula which Paul uses for matters he wants to emphasize. He always accompanies it with "brothers" (see Romans 1:13; 11:25; 1 Corinthians 10:1; 12:1; 2 Corinthians 1:8), as if it were a formula for sharing with friends a point he feels important. (Note: 1 Corinthians 11:3 and Colossians 2:1 look the same in translation, but they use a different Greek verb.) Here, the important fact concerns Christians **who have fallen asleep** (have died; 1 Thess. 4:14).

Sleep was a widely used metaphor for death among pagans, Jews, and Christians. It is common in both the Old and New Testaments (for example, Deuteronomy 31:16 KJV; 1 Kings 2:10 KJV; 22:40 KJV; John 11:11-13; Acts 7:60; 13:36; 1 Corinthians 11:30). For Christians, the comparison might suggest (1) rest after toil; (2) a separation which is only temporary; and (3) that there will be a time of awaking. But the fact that the metaphor was common also among those who do not believe in resurrection indicates that we should not make too much of such possible implications. But, given Christian belief, the term is appropriate.

Some Greek philosophers taught an immortality of the soul, and some of the contemporary "mystery religions" aimed to provide hope of life beyond death for their followers, but it was all rather vague and little understood by the general population. None of the Greeks believed in *bodily* resurrection. Leon Morris illustrates the difference between Christian and pagan reactions to death by citing two early papyri: "Irene to Taonnophris and Philo, good comfort. I was as sorry and wept over the departed one as I wept for Didymas. And all things whatsoever were fitting, I did. . . . But, nevertheless, against such things one can do nothing.

Therefore comfort ye one another."[3]   What an ironic closing line, in language like 1 Thessalonians 4:18, but so far removed in meaning.

In contrast, a letter from a Christian at about the same time describes their burial custom: "And if any righteous man among them passes from the world, they rejoice and offer thanks to God; and they escort the body as if he were setting out from one place to another near."[4]   Christians mourn the death of loved ones, of course, but they are also sustained by hope (see Matthew 5:4; Romans 12:15); theirs is not the bitter grief of permanent loss.   John Stott says, "Mourning is natural, even for a while emotionally necessary. . . . What Paul prohibits is not grief, but hopeless grief. . . ."[5]

Although untranslated in the New International Version, 4:14 begins with "For," indicating that Paul is giving the basis for the Christian hope.   Our confidence is not based on a philosophical reasoning or mystical intuition, but rather it rests on the solid foundation of the historical facts of Jesus' death and resurrection (1 Cor. 15:17-18).   The New International Version seeks to capture this emphasis with the words **and so** (1 Thess. 4:14).

Note Paul's words: **Jesus died** (4:14).   Paul does not say that Jesus "fell asleep."   He died, and "died for us" (5:10).   "He died that death which is the wages of sin; and because He endured the full horror implied in that death, He has transformed death for His followers into sleep."[6]   Christ's death was a real death, but it was also, as Puritan John Owen titled a book, *The Death of Death*.   The early seventeenth-century poet John Donne concluded his sonnet *Death Be Not Proud* with the lines, "One short sleep, we wake eternally, and death shall be no more; death, thou shalt die."[7]

Christ really died, but also He really rose again.   For the historical fact, there is a list of witnesses in 1 Corinthians 15:3-8.   For its theological implications, see, for example, 1 Corinthians 15:17-18; and compare verse 20, where "firstfruits" implies more fruit to follow later (see John 14:19; 1 Corinthians 6:14; 2 Corinthians 4:14).

On such a basis, Paul can reassure the Thessalonians **that God will bring with Jesus those who have fallen asleep in him** (1 Thess. 4:14). The resurrection of deceased Christians is not mentioned here explicitly, but the statement **that God will bring [them] with Jesus** clearly *implies* their resurrection, and Paul plainly states that they will return with Christ when He comes in His glory (4:14).   Paul develops this in verses 15 through 17.   The way these events are described here suggests that the Thessalonians' question was not about the *resurrection* of their loved ones. They were confident of that.   But they were not so sure about their participation in His parousia. The persons in view here are those who have fallen asleep in Him, which restricts the promise to Christians, of course. Probably the destiny of non-Christians is not discussed in this passage.

There has been much conjecture concerning the expression, the Lord's own word (4:15). It is generally agreed that **Lord,** standing here by itself, refers to Jesus. But the Gospels do not record such a saying.[8] Some think that Paul knew of an unrecorded word to this effect; others that he is summing up what he believes to be the thrust of Jesus' teaching; still others that he is claiming direct revelation (see Galatians 1:12; 1 Corinthians 15:51; Ephesians 3:3). In any case, whatever may be his source, by referring to the "Lord's own word," Paul makes his affirmation as authoritative as possible for the Thessalonians' reassurance.

We who are still alive (1 Thess. 4:15) has also prompted considerable discussion. Some have interpreted it as a declaration by Paul that the return of Christ will occur within Paul's lifetime. But such a flat assertion is unlikely. In the very next paragraph he indicates uncertainty ("whether we are awake or asleep" [5:10]). The expression here is more likely to be what I. Howard Marshall calls "the preacher's 'we,' by which he makes a statement applicable to both himself and to his hearers."[9] And he points out that in later writings Paul indicates the possibility, and even the likelihood, of his death before the Parousia (see 1 Corinthians 6:14; 2 Corinthians 4:14; 5:1; Philippians 1:20). Perhaps his expectations gradually changed over the years; that has been the experience of many older Christians.

And Paul declares emphatically (the Greek has a double negative) that those **who are left . . . will certainly not precede those who have fallen asleep** (1 Thess. 4:15). Some (for example, Marshall) think that, in this context, the Greek verb translated **precede** means not only going before others, but going before others in such a way as to gain an advantage. The fact that Paul felt it necessary to make this statement seems to indicate that the Thessalonians believed that those who had died would be at some sort of *disadvantage* in comparison with those still living at the time of Christ's coming. Paul corrects this misunderstanding, and by the double negative does so emphatically.

The **for** at the beginning of verse 16 indicates that Paul supports what he has just said by providing a fuller description of the Lord's coming. First, Christ will not be content to send a representative. **The Lord himself,** says Paul—He and no other—will return for His own, including **the dead** who belong to Him (4:16). Three phrases describe the scene, especially the "sound-effects": (1) there is **a loud command;** the term is used for the charioteer urging his horses or a ship's captain shouting to the rowers; it is thunderous and compelling; (2) there is **the voice of the archangel,** but in the Greek text there are no definite articles—no "the"— and thus we should read this "a voice of an archangel," or perhaps "a voice like an archangel's"; no particular archangel is named, but the voice has that awesome quality; and (3) there is **the trumpet call of God,** which is heard here as elsewhere in Scripture on occasions when God manifests His powerful presence (4:16; see Exodus 19:16; Isaiah 27:13; Joel 2:1; Zechariah 9:14; and see also 1 Corinthians 15:52; Matthew 24:31).

The three descriptive phrases may all refer to the same sound (see Revelation 1:10; 4:1), with the voice and the trumpet as the means by which the command is issued (see John 5:28-29). In any case, it certainly does not seem to describe a *"secret* rapture," in which Christians are snatched out of the world scene just before a great tribulation. It would be difficult to imagine anything more conspicuous.

Leon Morris cites J. B. Phillips' translation from *The New Testament in Modern English:* "One word of command, one shout from the archangel, one blast from the trumpet of God and the Lord himself will come down from Heaven!" and then adds, "Paul's main point is that it is none other than the Lord Himself who will come. The end of the age is not to be ushered in by some intermediary, but by God Himself (see Mic[ah] 1:3). The whole scene is awe-inspiring and full of grandeur."[10]

The powerful **voice** addresses, in the first instance, **the dead in Christ** (4:16), that is, those who lived and died as Christians. There is no information here concerning unbelievers or about the situation of Christians between their death and their resurrection. Here Paul reveals only what is needed to meet the Thessalonians' special anxieties concerning their deceased (Christian) loved ones. *They* will rise first, that is, first in relation to living Christians (1 Corinthians 15:50-52 gives some light on the transformation of the living). Thus the Thessalonians are assured that their deceased loved ones will participate fully in the events surrounding the return of Christ. In fact, they will precede living Christians and thus have a certain momentary advantage.

The next stage, as indicated by **after that** (1 Thess. 4:17), now brings into the picture Christians living at the time of Christ's return. They **will be caught up together with** those who were deceased (4:17). The Greek verb is a strong one; it could be translated "snatched up" suddenly and powerfully. The same verb describes the Roman soldiers rescuing Paul from the near riot in the Jewish council chamber (Acts 23:10); the rescue of the male child from the red dragon (Rev. 12:5); Philip's being carried away after the conversion of the Ethiopian eunuch (Acts 8:39); and Paul's mysterious experience of being caught up to the third heaven (2 Cor. 12:2, 4).

The scene Paul attempts to sketch exceeds our imagination. It is difficult to bring all the diverse elements into one consistent picture. I. Howard Marshall observes, "A real event is being described, but it is one which cannot be described literally since the direct activity of God cannot be fully comprehended in human language."[11]

John Stott offers helpful comments: "We know from Jesus himself that his coming will be personal, visible and glorious, but we also know that it will not be local ('There he is!' 'Here he is!') but universal ('like the lightning which flashes and lights the sky from one end to the other'). Presumably, therefore, our going to meet him will also transcend space. As for the *clouds,* they are to every Bible reader a familiar and easily recognized symbol of the immediate presence of God."[12]

In fact, the clouds may have an additional function. In the light of Daniel 7:13, they may be the *vehicle* conveying the "one like a son of man" into the presence of the Ancient of Days (see Mark 13:26; 14:62; Acts 1:9; Revelation 1:7).

To meet the Lord in the air (1 Thess. 4:17) raises further questions of interpretation. Generally, in biblical times, **the air** referred to the space between earth and the heavens. But then what? Those who are **caught up** (4:17) can hardly remain suspended there. Do they accompany Jesus back to heaven, or do they join Him and "all his holy ones" (3:13) as they descend to the earth? The word for **meet** may shed some light. The Greek means, more literally, "for a meeting," and the word which occurs here was often used to describe a delegation of local leaders going to meet a distinguished visitor to honor him by escorting him back to the city. Thus, in the New Testament, it describes the virgins meeting the bridegroom (Matt. 25:6) and the Roman disciples meeting Paul (Acts 28:15-16). In those instances, the delegation going to meet the arriving party then turned around after the meeting and accompanied the visitor to his destination.

Does this mean that the great host of Christians will rise to meet Jesus in the air and then become part of His triumphal procession to earth (Rev. 19:14)? I. Howard Marshall thinks that "we may well take the further step of deducing that the Lord's people go to meet him in order to escort him back to earth. . . ."[13] On the other hand, Charles Wanamaker is equally confident that we can fairly conclude, on the basis of 1 Thessalonians 4:17b, that "both living and dead Christians will return to heaven with the Lord. . . ."[14] F. F. Bruce judges, "It cannot be determined from what is said here whether the Lord (with his people) continues his journey to earth or returns to heaven."[15] Perhaps there is a warning here against overconfident building of end-time schemes.

In any case, what is most important is that **we will be with the Lord forever** (4:17). The climax has been reached. Many unanswered questions remain, but this is all we need to know: we shall be with Christ, reunited with loved ones, and together with all the people of God forever.

Paul concludes this paragraph with a practical application: **Therefore encourage each other with these words** (4:18). The word translated **encourage** also means "comfort," and that is perhaps more appropriate in this context. In any case, when friends are bereaved, we often feel that our words, intended to comfort, are wholly inadequate. But here we have **the Lord's own word** (4:15). Leon Morris says, "Whether we live, or whether we die, we do not go beyond His power; and in the face of death, that antagonist no man can master, we can yet remain calm and triumphant, for we know that those who sleep sleep in Jesus, and that there is a place for them in the final scheme of things."[16]

2. ASSURANCE FOR THE LIVING 5:1-11

One could say that in 1 Thessalonians 4:13-18 Paul addresses himself to Thessalonian ignorance—specifically, to a gap in their knowledge concerning deceased believers' participation in Christ's parousia. But now, in 5:1-11, he speaks to what they **know** (5:2).

In this segment, the purpose will not be to provide new information, but rather to remind and reassure the Thessalonians concerning what Paul has already taught them orally. He begins with what he acknowledges to be an unnecessary reminder: They know that the Day of the Lord will come as a surprise, suddenly and inescapably (5:1-3). They also know themselves to be **sons of the day,** and understand the appropriate lifestyle (5:4-8). Furthermore, and even more basic, they know that their hope of salvation rests ultimately on the saving purpose of God manifested in the atoning death of Christ (5:9-10). And on that basis, they can give and receive mutual encouragement and minister to one another (5:11).

The tone of this section is one of reassurance, as if the Thessalonians are somewhat apprehensive and unsure of their status before God. Probably, like most Christians in this first generation of the church, they expect the return of Christ soon, very likely in their own lifetime. How will they fare? Notice how Paul reassures them: **Destruction will come on *them*. . . . You are sons of the day. . . . God did not appoint *us* to suffer wrath but to. . .**

live together with him. Therefore encourage one another. . . . (5:3-11, my emphasis). In this section, too, we may see Paul's pastoral touch.

This new section begins in the standard pattern of this letter: he addresses them as **brothers** (5:1), and indicates the topic. Or, in this case, first he mentions what he will *not* be discussing—**times and dates** (5:1). These two nearly synonymous terms, especially when together like this, were a traditional expression for the Day of the Lord (see below), as the parallel in the next verse shows (see Daniel 2:21; Mark 13:32; Acts 1:7).

It is possible that the Thessalonians have been asking for signs of Christ's return so that they could be sure to be ready. Paul answers that on this topic there is no **need to write** (1 Thess. 5:1). He has already told them all they need to know and, for that matter, perhaps all he himself knows. Therefore, he now can only remind them briefly of what he has already taught them. After all, Jesus himself said that He did not know "that day or hour" (Mark 13:32), and later, even after His resurrection, He had told the apostles, "It is not for you to know the times or dates the Father has set by his own authority" (Acts 1:7). It remains true, as Jesus said: "The Son of Man will come at an hour when you do not expect him." (Matt. 24:44).

Of course, that does not seem to keep many persons from speculation. As I. Howard Marshall remarks, "It is worth observing that many people today crave detailed information about both the time and the course of the last events, and there are writers who are prepared to answer the question in minute detail and with not a little imagination. . . . Not so Paul. . . . Christian teachers today would do well to follow his example and so avoid 'going beyond what is written' (1 Cor[inthians] 4:6, literal rendering)."[17]

The text before us explains why Paul says **we do not need to write** (1 Thess. 5:1). For what they *need* to know, they know already—that **the day of the Lord will come like a thief in the night** (5:2). The Day of the Lord is, of course, a rather common Old Testament expression for the future occasion when God will establish His righteousness on the earth, including both judgment of the wicked (see Isaiah 13:6-16; Joel 1:15; Amos 5:18-20) and full deliverance for His people (see Joel 2:31-32; Obadiah 15-21; Zechariah 14). The same expression conveying the same two aspects is carried over into the New Testament, with some variations of terminology: for example, "that day" (Luke 10:12), "the day" (2 Thess. 1:10), "the day the Son of Man" (Luke 17:30); "the coming of the Son of Man" (Matt. 24:27, 37, 39); "the day of our Lord Jesus Christ" (1 Cor. 1:8; see 2 Corinthians 1:14; Philippians 1:6, 10; 2:16).

It is worth noting that the Greek verb translated **will come** (1 Thess. 5:2) is actually in the present tense; thus, it means literally, "comes." This gives a certain vividness and certainty to the whole idea. It says the event is already on the way. (The same is true of **will come** in verse 3.) The implication of **like a thief** (5:2) is first of all unexpectedness, but perhaps also loss for those who are not prepared. The intention is to call for vigilance, as in Luke 12:39-40 (see Revelation 3:3; 16:15). The basic idea is found in several places in the New Testament, but this is the only setting where the phrase **in the night** is added (1 Thess. 5:2). Leon Morris comments, "The addition completes the picture of a totally unheralded approach, devastating in its unexpectedness." He adds, "This does away with all date fixing."[18]

While people are saying, "Peace and safety" (1 Thess. 5:3) reflects Old Testament descriptions of false prophets predicting peace and security when, in fact, divine judgment was on the way (see Jeremiah 6:13-15; 8:11; Ezekiel 13:10-16; Micah 3:5). The comparison of **labor pains** (1 Thess. 5:3) and divine judgment occurs repeatedly in the Old Testament (Isa. 13:6-8; Jer. 4:31; 22:23; Mic. 4:10; and see Mark 13:8). According to F. F. Bruce, "The point of comparison is the sudden onset of labor pains with their inescapable outcome."[19] If the thief-in-the-night picture emphasizes the unexpectedness, the woman-in-childbirth analogy underlines the certainty; the process is in motion ("comes") and there is no escaping it.

Paul turns from the basic facts which the Thessalonians know very well (1 Thess. 5:2), to reassuring words about who they are and what they know (5:4). And from this point on there is reiterated distinction between two groups of people. There are the people **of the light** (5:5), starting out as **you** in verses 4 and 5, but becoming **we** or **us** in verses 5, 6, 8, 9 and 10. Then there are the people of **the darkness—they** in verses 3 and 7 (see 5b, 6a, 9a). In addition to the contrast between darkness and night, and between light and day, Paul also makes use of the further distinction between sleeping and watchfulness, and between drunkenness and sobriety. These are natural comparisons/contrasts, found rather frequently in both the Old and New Testaments, and common in Judaism at that time.[20] The Thessalonian Christians know—or should know—which side they are on, and, therefore, they do not need to be anxious and fearful, even though Christ's return will be sudden and unexpected.

Again naming them as family, **brothers** (and sisters; 5:4), Paul reinforces the reason why they should not be anxious to know times and dates, or fear the coming of Christ as though He were **a thief in the night**

(5:2): *they* **are not in darkness** (5:4). **Not in darkness** implies they do not live and move and have their being there. The coming of Christ will surprise them, but will not bring loss and destruction.

Paul next supports this positive affirmation in verse 5, which begins with a "for" that is not translated in the New International Version. He reminds his readers, **You are all sons of the light,** and here he uses another common biblical mode of expression. To be the "son of something" meant to be especially characterized by that thing, as Jesus nicknamed James and John "Sons of Thunder" (Mark 3:17) and described Judas as "the son of perdition" (John 17:12 Revised Standard Version). Paul also refers to "the sons of disobedience" in Ephesians 2:2 (RSV). Thus, Paul here describes the Thessalonian Christians as not only walking in the light, but, on a deeper level, being characterized by light, inwardly and essentially. They are people of integrity and, therefore, can be perfectly open about everything; they can be totally transparent.

And **sons of the day** is an even stronger statement (1 Thess. 5:5). The **day,** of course, is the occasion at the end of history when God fully manifests himself in power and glory, judgment and salvation. Although the Day of the Lord has not yet occurred, **sons of the day** are those who long for that day, and when it arrives they will not seek to flee from its light. They are not afraid to be seen for who they are; their character matches the pure white light of God's day.

Leon Morris says, "Believers find in the Day of the Lord a situation in which they are perfectly at home. Just as the light is their characteristic, so also is participation in the glorious events of the Day of the Lord."[21] Believers have "tasted . . . the powers of the coming age" and responded to God's call "out of darkness into his wonderful light" (see Hebrews 6:5; 1 Peter 2:9). They are on their way to becoming "blameless and pure, children of God without fault in a crooked and depraved generation, in which you shine like stars in the universe" (see Philippians 2:15).

Paul reinforces this description by stating the truth in negative form: **We do *not* belong to the night or to the darkness** (1 Thess. 5:5b, my emphasis). In a context like this, **night** suggests alienation from God, and **darkness** is the realm of sin and iniquity. We may note in passing that **belong to the night** is a stronger expression than being **in darkness** (5:4a). Those who are content to remain *in* the darkness may eventually find themselves *owned* by it.

Verses 4 and 5 serve as a sort of bridge between the indication of the Thessalonians' anxiety (5:1-3) and direct exhortation (5:6-11); and, in the process, Paul switches from **you** to **we** or **us.** This is a sound pastoral approach because, in this way, he includes himself among those who must put into practice the implications of the truth he has been enunciating. The exhortation that follows rests upon the truth just stated. This is made clear by the strong expression of consequence or result which begins in verse 6 with **So then.**

The next verses continue the running contrast between the people **of the light** and the people of **the darkness** (5:5). The people of the night are described as **asleep** (5:6). This is a different application of the comparison with sleeping from verse 4, where it was used for death. Here in verse 7, **sleep** indicates carelessness or indifference. It means being in a condition in which one is unaware, unconscious of what is happening, especially in the realm of spiritual realities. It is not being **alert** (5:6) and is, therefore, like the householder who did not protect his house from the thief (Luke 12:39), or the servant unprepared for the returning master (Mark 13:36; see Ephesians 5:14).

Then, carrying the idea of belonging to the **night** in another direction, Paul mentions that nighttime rather than day, characteristically, is when people are more likely to become drunk (see Acts 2:15). Becoming drunk indicates recklessness, the opposite of being "self-controlled," and is perhaps worse than being **asleep.** One can waken from sleep quickly, but recovering from a drunken stupor requires time. One is "out of action" longer. Being **asleep** might represent so-called sins of omission (for example, prayerlessness), while drunkenness would resemble the so-called sins of commission (for example, an addiction to pornography).

In verse 8, the **we** is emphatic, strongly contrasting with the **others** of verses 6 and 7. The people **of the light** are to be **alert** (5:5-6); vigilant (a word common in such contexts; for example, three times in Mark 13:34-37); and **self-controlled** (1 Thess. 5:6)—literally *sober,* in contrast to being drunk. A. L. Moore says, "[The word] denotes serious, responsible moral behavior, as drunkenness denotes abandonment of self-control and responsibility."[22] Paul uses the Greek word again in 1 Corinthians 15:34 and 2 Timothy 4:5 (see 1 Peter 1:13; 4:7; 5:8).

The occurrence of **self-controlled** again in 1 Thessalonians 5:8 leads into another set of word pictures drawn from military life. The connection between sobriety and Christian armor is not obvious. Perhaps Paul moves from the idea of vigilance to the thought of a sentry on duty, alert and well-armed (see a similar progression of thought in Romans 13:11-13; the general thought may have been prompted by Isaiah 59:17). Paul has a bit of problem because he has two items of armor and three virtues to encourage. Later he will work it out more fully (Eph. 6:13-18), but now he wants to urge the familiar triad—**faith, love, hope**—as qualities necessary for being prepared for Christ's return (1 Thess. 5:8). **Faith** and **love** as a breastplate will protect vital organs, heart and lungs. The **hope of salvation as a helmet,** protecting the head, is in the climactic position (5:8). **Hope** is especially appropriate in a context of waiting for the Second Coming.

For in verse 9 indicates that Paul is giving the basis for our **hope of salvation.** That **hope** is not misplaced because, as the word **appoint** indicates, it rests upon the sovereign purpose of God (5:9). The initiative is His, for He has "chosen us" (1:4), "from the beginning" (2 Thess. 2:13; see Ephesians 1:4). And that eternal purpose He puts into action in our lives as He "calls" us (1 Thess. 2:12; 4:7; 5:24).

At the same time, our human responsibility is indicated here by **receive**(4:9), a word which I. Howard Marshall thinks Paul used "because he wants to bring out the need for Christians to play their part in receiving salvation. . . . He does not suggest that God's plan is fulfilled independently of the action of man." Marshall adds, "Paul's exhortations to vigilance would be nonsensical if vigilance was the product of some inward causation in the believer by God or if there was no possibility of disobeying the exhortation."[23]

In the latter part of the quotation, Marshall is referring to extreme views of predestination of the kind popularly referred to as "once in grace, *always in grace.*" In our reaction to that extreme, we must not go to the other. Finally, our **hope of salvation** does rest on God's faithfulness (5:9, 24).

Paul's emphasis here is upon what God has done for our **salvation;** *that* is the basis of our confidence, rather than the constancy we can muster. Our **salvation** is through our Lord Jesus Christ, a phrase Paul also uses elsewhere to direct his readers' attention to the basis of salvation: God saves through Jesus Christ, our Lord and Savior.

He died for us (5:10) points to the basis of our salvation through our Lord Jesus Christ—Christ's atoning death for us and our union with Him by faith. The little phrase **for us** must not be missed. It expresses the truth of substitutionary atonement, which, of course, is basic in Pauline theology (Rom. 3:21-26; 5:6, 8; 8:3; 2 Cor. 5:14-15; etc.). The way he mentions it here, almost in passing, indicates that he had made that a basic element in his teaching of the new believers in Thessalonica (1 Thess. 1:10; 2:15; 4:14); therefore, he does not need to elaborate now.

In **whether we are awake or asleep** (1 Thess. 5:10), Paul returns to his first application of **asleep** as picturing death (see 4:14). In 5:6, we noticed, he used the term to represent a careless indifference, the opposite of being **alert.** And after his strong emphasis on the necessity of watchfulness in verses 6 and 7, he certainly would not, almost immediately, suggest that it was not important to stay **alert** because, in any case, God will grant us life with Him.

All interpreters agree that in verse 10, Paul means that **whether we are awake** (that is, living) **or asleep** (that is, deceased), God will take us to be with Him forever. Thus, nearing the close of the section on the return of Christ, Paul reassures both those concerned about deceased loved ones and those apprehensive about their own destiny, that Christ has conquered sin and death. Therefore, we may hold fast to our **hope of salvation** (5:8) because Christ has fast hold on *all* who are His own.

Of course, this is no excuse for coasting along carelessly in our Christian lives. Rather, the conclusion Paul draws is this: **Therefore encourage one another** (5:11). This is the same Greek verb as that used in 4:18, but now the emphasis is upon mutual exhortation, on encouraging more than comforting. This is clear from the context, and is supported by the use of the second verb of exhortation—**build each other up** (5:11). The latter is a favorite theme of Paul (1 Cor. 8:1; 10:24; 14:3-5, 12, 17, 26; Eph. 4:12, 16, 29; 2 Cor. 10:8; 12:19; 13:10). Both verbs are in a form which denotes continuous action. Thus, J. B. Phillips translates 5:11, "So go on cheering and strengthening each other . . ." *(The New Testament in Modern English).*

We should notice the mutuality connected with both commands: **encourage one another and build each other up** (1 Thess. 5:11a). *Every* believer has something to contribute to the other members of the body of Christ. Later Paul will elaborate on this (1 Cor. 12). But already, in this which may be his earliest letter, he is emphasizing the importance of "body life." We may think of Paul as the intrepid pioneer missionary, but he was no "lone ranger."

Just as in fact you are doing (1 Thess. 5:11) illustrates once more Paul's tactfulness and his use of positive reinforcement, marks of a good pastor.

So Paul closes this section by calling for mutual ministry within the body. What form(s) should that ministry take? He provides some direction in the next paragraph.

ENDNOTES

[1]William Barclay, *A New Testament Wordbook* (New York: Harper and Brothers, Publishers, n.d.), p. 91.

[2]Ernest Best, *A Commentary of the First and Second Epistles to the*

Thessalonians, Harper's New Testament Commentaries (New York: Harper and Row Publishers, 1972), pp. 180–81.

[3]Leon Morris, *The Epistles of Paul to the Thessalonians,* Tyndale New Testament Commentary (Grand Rapids, Michigan: Wm. B. Eerdmans Publishing Co., 1957), p. 84.

[4]Ibid., p. 85.

[5]John Stott, *The Gospel and the End of Time* (Downers Grove, Illinois: InterVarsity Press, 1991), p. 91.

[6]Morris, p. 85.

[7]John Donne, in *The Selected Poetry of John Donne* by Marius Bewley (New York: New American Library, 1966), p. 270.

[8]The Gospels include the New Testament books of Matthew, Mark, Luke, and John.

[9]I. Howard Marshall, *1 and 2 Thessalonians,* New Century Bible Commentary (Grand Rapids, Michigan: Wm. B. Eerdmans Publishing Co., 1983), p. 127.

[10]Morris, p. 87.

[11]Marshall, p. 128.

[12]Stott, p. 104.

[13]Marshall, p. 131.

[14]Charles A. Wanamaker, *The Epistles to the Thessalonians,* New International Greek Testament Commentary (Grand Rapids, Michigan: Wm. B. Eerdmans Publishing Co., 1990), p. 175.

[15]F. F. Bruce, *1 and 2 Thessalonians,* Word Biblical Commentary (Waco, Texas: Word Books, Publisher, 1982), p. 103.

[16]Morris, p. 89.

[17]Marshall, pp. 132–33.

[18]Leon Morris, *The First and Second Epistles to the Thessalonians,* rev. ed., New International Commentary on the New Testament (Grand Rapids, Michigan: Wm. B. Eerdmans Publishing Co., 1991), p. 151.

[19]Bruce, p. 110.

[20]Judaism is the life and belief system of the Jewish people and involves a covenant relationship with God. Though there are various branches of Judaism, the underlying theme among them is monotheism and a recognition of the Law, or the Torah (the first five books of the Old Testament: Genesis, Exodus, Leviticus, Numbers, and Deuteronomy).

[21]Morris, *The First and Second Epistles to the Thessalonians,* p. 155.

[22]A. L. Moore, *1 and 2 Thessalonians,* Century Bible (London: Thomas Nelson and Sons, Ltd., 1969), p. 76.

[23]Marshall, p. 139.

5

PRESENT: CONGREGATIONAL DUTIES

1 Thessalonians 5:12-24

The preceding section on the second coming of Christ (1 Thess. 4:13–5:11) fell into two subdivisions: assurance to bereaved Christians that the dead in Christ would fully participate in the parousia of Christ (4:13-18); and encouragement for believers who were anxious about the unexpectedness of Christ's return, by reassuring them of their appointment by God for salvation through Christ (5:1-11). Both paragraphs closed with admonitions to mutual comfort, encouragement, and edification within the body of Christ at Thessalonica (4:18; 5:11).

We may fairly deduce from this that Paul believed the best environment in which to wait for the coming of Christ to be the Christian community which we call the local church. To make sure of that for the Thessalonians, in this next and final section of the letter Paul and his colleagues provide some guiding principles for strengthening their congregational life. It is noticeable that we are told very little about any organizational structure. In fact, although there are recognized leaders (5:12), most of the exhortations seem to apply to the congregation as a whole.

There is no indication that matters were in a crisis state, nor any evidence of an acute problem in any particular aspect of congregational life. It would be a mistake to engage in what some interpreters call "mirror-reading"—taking each specific injunction as proof that its opposite was presently occurring in the life of the church. For example, it would be mirror-reading to judge, on the basis of an exhortation to a congregation to love one another, that the church was experiencing bitter division.

Most of the instructions in the passage before us, 5:12-24, are just the sort an experienced missionary-pastor would address to almost any young congregation. The possible exception would be the problem of idleness (5:14; see 4:11); by the time Paul writes the Thessalonians again, severe disciplinary action will be required (2 Thess. 3:6-13). Most of the admonitions in 1 Thessalonians address very basic aspects of personal and congregational Christian living. One indication that this is not "advanced" or specialized instruction is that many of the directions given here parallel passages from both the teachings of Jesus and from other New Testament letters (for example, Romans 12). So these are basic aspects of Christian discipleship, but not less significant on that account. From this training program, no one "graduates."

The instructions here are varied in character and, at first appearance, seem somewhat miscellaneous. It is not easy to perceive a pattern. But perhaps the following analysis will suffice for present purposes: social (or interpersonal) duties (5:12-15); spiritual (or religious) duties (5:16-22); prayer for sanctification (5:23-24). The last subsection, the prayer of verses 23 and 24, *could* be joined with the conclusion in verses 25 through 28. It does link with it, of course, but it seems more closely knit to the preceding set of admonitions. It brings the main division (4:1–5:24) to a close in a manner parallel to the way in which the prayer of 3:11-13 crowns the first main division.

1. SOCIAL DUTIES 5:12-15

Paul alerts the Thessalonians to his new topic in the usual fashion with **Now** and **brothers** (1 Thess. 5:12), as in earlier sections of the letter. **Brothers** occurs twice at the beginning of this section (1 Thess. 5:12-14) and three times more at the very close (5:25-27). Perhaps there is more than habit at work here. As he begins this set of instructions on their life together, there well may be in the back of Paul's mind the imagery of the church as God's family (see Galatians 6:10; Ephesians 2:19). But if so, he does not linger over the point, but rather plunges right into the matter at hand.

First, in any human organization, however democratic it intends to be, there must be some sort of leadership. Acts 14:23 illustrates the practice of Paul and his colleagues; they made sure that young congregations had recognized leaders. Frequently they were called *elders*, a term borrowed from the Jewish synagogue. Usually there were several elders, rather than the one-pastor/one-congregation pattern common today. In the predominantly Gentile Thessalonian church, the pattern may have been a little different, perhaps modeled after their trade guilds or social organizations.

But leaders there were. And they are described as performing three functions: they **work,** they **are over,** they **admonish** (1 Thess. 5:12). The first term indicates the strenuous nature of their labors. Paul used another form of the same word to point to their own physical labor to maintain themselves there in Thessalonica (2:9). He also uses it to describe his ministerial labors (see 1 Corinthians 15:10; Colossians 1:29). He indicates how much energy pastoral ministering may require: "So I will very gladly spend for you everything I have and expend myself as well" (2 Cor. 12:15a).

Exactly what is intended by the leaders being **over** the congregation (1 Thess. 5:12) is unclear. The word is used for "exercising leadership" or " presiding," and also for "caring for," "protecting," or "sharing with." F. F. Bruce thinks that both aspects of the term apply, and thus here it "combines the ideas of leading, protecting, and caring for."[1] That the qualifying phrase **in the Lord** (5:12) is attached to this specific aspect of their leadership is significant, for it indicates, on one hand, the *basis* of their authority—they are there by His appointment—and, on the other, the *limits* of their authority—their leadership is to be exercised in the style taught and exemplified by Jesus (see Mark 10:42-45). In this way only are they to be "over" their brothers and sisters. They do not *own* the flock, but are under-shepherds, who eventually will have to give account to the "Chief Shepherd" (see 1 Peter 5:1-4). The flock is so precious to Him that He laid down His life for them (see John 10:11-17).

The third aspect of the leaders' ministry is to **admonish** (1 Thess. 5:12). The word calls for instructing with a view to changing behavior. It involves "correcting" people, but doing so in a manner which does not alienate, but rather maintains rapport, keeps the door open for further guidance. A chief means of guidance is to lead by example (1 Pet. 5:3); like the Apostle Paul, they need to be able to say to the congregation, "Follow my example, as I follow the example of Christ" (1 Cor. 11:1).

First Thessalonians 5:12 is addressed to the congregation (**brothers**). Paul sets forth their responsibility to the leaders who work, preside, and admonish. They are, in the first place, to "acknowledge" them, that is to say, to recognize their leaders' proper role. "Acknowledge" is perhaps more accurate than the New International Version's **respect,** since **respect** is more nearly the thrust of verse 13. So the congregation *begins* by "acknowledging" their leaders, but beyond that, they are to **hold them in the highest regard** (5:13; or "esteem them very highly" [New Revised

Standard Version]). And they are to do so, not grudgingly nor dutifully, but **in love,** and in grateful appreciation for their work (5:13). Leon Morris comments, "It is a matter of fact that to this day we are often slow to realize that effective leadership in the church of Christ demands effective following. If we are continually critical of those who are set over us in the Lord, small wonder that they are unable to perform the miracles that we demand of them."[2]

When leaders recognize their responsibility to lead "in the Lord" and keenly feel their accountability to Him, and at the same time the congregation responds with respect, affection, and appreciation, then life in the Christian community is more likely to be characterized by peace. Still, that does not happen automatically; it requires vigilance, sensitivity, and mutual commitment. Therefore, Paul's instruction comes in the form of a command: **Live in peace with each other** (5:13b). This sort of exhortation to peace is frequent in the New Testament (see Mark 9:50; Romans 12:18; 2 Corinthians 13:11; Ephesians 4:3; 2 Timothy 2:22; James 3:18; and see Romans 15:5; Philippians 2:2; 4:2. Apparently this matter required emphasis then, even as it does today. It is a "fruit of the Spirit" (Gal. 5:22), but it requires cultivating.

There has been some debate over identifying which **brothers** are addressed in verse 14. The duties that follow—**warn, encourage, help,** etc.—could well apply specifically to the elders. But most interpreters hold that Paul continues to address the congregation at large: because throughout this letter, **brothers** has referred to the whole congregation (1:4; 2:1, 9, 14, 17; 4:1, 13; 5:1, 4, 12, 25); and because, if he were changing from the brothers addressed in verse 12 to another set of brothers in verse 14, the verse should begin with a strong form of But rather than **And,** and the **you** should be more emphatic. Therefore, as I. Howard Marshall observes, "The succeeding exhortations . . . are meant for the whole church. For Paul the whole church was involved in mutual care, and not just a group of leaders."[3] What Paul is doing, and *intends* to do, is "to give the whole community a sense of pastoral responsibility."[4]

The congregation as a whole, then, is urged to be ready to help three categories of persons (5:14): (1) the **idle,** literally "those out of line," but the use of the term in 2 Thessalonians 3:6-15 (see 1 Thessalonians 4:11) seems to indicate idleness as their specific problem; they need someone to warn them—as irresponsible, undisciplined, they need to be told to mend their ways; (2) the **timid,** the anxious and fearful—perhaps because of persecution, anxiety about the Second Coming, or feelings of inadequacy; they need someone to encourage them, bolster them, reassure them, make them feel that they count; and (3) the **weak,** perhaps easily led astray, morally or spiritually (1 Cor. 8:9-13; Rom. 14–15:13)— they need someone to help, that is, someone to take hold of them and give support. James Denney urges taking this seriously: "Men and women slip away and are lost to the Church and to Christ, because they were weak and no one supported them. Your word or your influence, spoken or used at the right time, might have saved them. What is the use of strength if not to lay hold of the weak?"[5]

The whole congregation is called to accept responsibility for the whole congregation, even if sometimes we would rather not bear the weight of such responsibility. Furthermore, many will say, "Where does one draw the line?" Some may even say, "In 4:11 Paul directed us to lead a quiet life, and mind our own business." Perhaps Paul would respond, "Looking out for friends, neighbors, fellow Christians, anyone in need, *is* your business." Obviously, finding a proper balance is required. But it may be too easy to "let ourselves off the hook."

First Thessalonians 5:14 concludes with the call to **be patient with everyone,** but it will be especially necessary with the kinds of people just described. Patience is a mark of love. Help offered in a reluctant, resentful frame of mind may even be counterproductive, not truly beneficial in the long run. The help may be accepted, but the recipient is alienated in the process. John Stott declares, "We have no excuse for becoming impatient with them on the ground that they are difficult, demanding, disappointing, argumentative or rude. On the contrary, we are to be *patient* with all of them. *Makrothymia* [patience], often translated 'long-suffering,' is an attribute of God (Ps[alm] 103:8), a fruit of the Spirit (Gal[atians] 5:22), and a characteristic of love (1 Cor[inthians] 13:4)."[6]

And the exercise of patience includes, among many other things, no retaliation: **nobody pays back wrong for wrong** (1 Thess. 5:15). Revenge is ruled out, in the first place, because it is forbidden by the Lord (see Matthew 5:43-48; 7:12; Luke 6:27; also Romans 12:17-21; 1 Peter 3:9). But also, as a violation of the law of love, it is detrimental to the common life of the congregation, even if it only takes the form of secretly holding a grudge. It may require vigilance, as the words **make sure** imply (1 Thess. 5:15); the desire to get even is almost instinctive to fallen human nature. Sometimes it seems so *deserved.* But, "Do not take revenge, my friends, but leave room for God's wrath, for it is written: 'It is mine to avenge; I will repay,' says the Lord" (Rom. 12:19).

So, restraining our natural feelings, we must rather always try to be kind. But try is too weak a translation here; the Greek means to "seek eagerly";

the word is often translated *pursue,* as of a hunter after game. What one should be seeking is the opportunity to serve one another. Furthermore, the form of the verb signifies continuous action, and also the command is further strengthened by **always** (1 Thess. 5:15). And, making the requirement even more difficult, this is to be our consistent attitude, not only within the Christian community (**each other**), but also toward outsiders (**everyone else**).

F. F. Bruce describes the vision of church life here: "The Christian community is to be a little welfare state, a society practicing mutual aid among its members in spiritual and material respects. Within its fellowship those who need help should be given the help they need. A special responsibility in this regard rests on the leaders of the community, but it is a ministry in which all can have some share."[7] There may be undertones in Bruce's language here which arouse concern. But if our first and *only* reaction is, "People will take advantage," perhaps we need to contemplate the vision longer.

2. RELIGIOUS DUTIES 5:16-22

The preceding section dealt with interpersonal relations with respect to both fellow Christians and outsiders; this paragraph deals with spiritual aspects of the common life within the Christian fellowship. Some are primarily matters of personal piety; others pertain to congregational worship. The instructions seem to fall into two subdivisions: three parallel commands which are more personal and inward, all of which are described as **God's will for you** (5:16-18); and then five more exhortations, all apparently dealing with the role of the Spirit and His gifts in the life of the congregation (5:19-22).

Be joyful always (5:16) is a common New Testament theme (see Romans 12:12-15; 2 Corinthians 6:10; Philippians 2:18; 3:1; 4:4), often in settings in which the context is hardship and persecution (for example, 1 Thessalonians 1:6; see Matthew 5:10-12; 1 Peter 4:13; Acts 5:41; 16:25; John 16:21-22). On this last point, Leon Morris quotes W. A. Visser't Hooft: "It is one of the impressive aspects of the life of the Church in history that the churches under pressure or under persecution know so much more about the secret of Christian joy than the churches which live in the circumstances of tranquillity."[8]

Joy is contagious, of course, and beneficial for Christians themselves. But joy also makes the Christian life attractive to others. The principal resource for living a joy-filled life is the clear sense of the nearness of

Christ, even in the midst of adverse circumstances. This leads naturally to the next instruction.

Pray continually is another common New Testament theme (1 Thess. 5:17; see, for example, Romans 12:12; Ephesians 6:18; Colossians 4:2), and Paul affirms this as his own practice (1 Thess. 1:2; Rom. 1:9-10; Eph. 1:16; Col. 1:9; 2 Thess. 1:11). This means being in prayer not only at appointed times, but *always*—always at least in the sense that one never consciously stops praying, as if somehow, in that moment, he were not dependent upon God. **Continually** needs to be understood in a reasonable way. "Though it is quite impossible for us to be always uttering words of prayer, it is possible and necessary that we should always be living in the spirit of prayer."[9]

But beyond permeating our own lives with prayer, as congregations we should also give ourselves to systematic intercession. John Stott says, "We should be praying for our own church members, far and near; for the church throughout the world, its leaders, its adherence to the truth of God's revelation, its holiness, unity and mission; for our nation, parliament and government, and for a just, free, compassionate and participatory society; for world mission, especially for places and people resistant to the gospel; for peace, justice and environmental stewardship; and for the poor, the oppressed, the hungry, the homeless and the sick."[10]

Like the other two, the third instruction in this group is also a common biblical theme: **give thanks in all circumstances** (1 Thess. 5:18; see Ephesians 5:20; Philippians 4:6; Colossians 2:7; 3:15, 17; 4:2; 1 Timothy 4:3-5); and again Paul's own practice (1 Thess. 1:2; 2:13; Rom. 1:8; 1 Cor. 1:4). Such gratitude even in difficult circumstances arises from our recognition of the sovereignty of God and His providence in our lives. He is in control, and He is mindful of His own (see Matthew 10:29-31). We see His hand in everything which impacts our lives; or, if we cannot *see*, we *trust*. We are confident that our loving Heavenly Father gives only good gifts to His children (see Matthew 7:9-11; James 1:17-18). This is the opposite of the sin of murmuring, which so often brought judgment upon ancient Israel.

As **for** indicates, **this is God's will for you in Christ Jesus** provides the basic motivation and the divine enabling for obedience to these three commands (1 Thess. 5:18). The expression **God's will** may be taken in two ways here: (1) these are what God requires; and (2) these are what God intends and what His grace makes possible—a devotional life marked by joy, prayerfulness, and gratitude, because and insofar as we are in Christ Jesus. Jesus *models* the life of joy, prayerfulness, and thanksgiving, as we see set before us in the Gospels.[11] Indwelling our lives through the Spirit, He *empowers* such a life in those who live and move and have their being in Him.

John Wesley warmly endorsed this threefold description of the Christian life. After describing prayer as the "fruit" of rejoicing, and thanksgiving as the "fruit" of both rejoicing and prayer, he declares, "This is Christian perfection. Further than this we cannot go; and we need not stop short of it."[12]

In 1 Thessalonians 5:19-22, Paul issues five more commands in quick succession. The first two are negative, and the form of the verb probably implies that the activities mentioned are, in fact, taking place among the Thessalonians. The last three are positive; they could be quite general in meaning, but most interpreters connect them rather closely with the first two. In that case, all five instructions here deal with the place of the Spirit and His gifts in congregational life. On close examination, we notice that the second instruction is one aspect of the first; the fourth and fifth are positive and negative aspects of the third.

Do not put out the Spirit's fire (5:19). Obviously, this is based on picturing the Spirit as fire (Matt. 3:11; Acts 2:3). In other passages, Christians are urged to be "aglow with the Spirit" (Rom. 12:11 Revised Standard Version), and Timothy is encouraged to "fan into flame the gift of God" (2 Tim. 1:6); in both cases the immediately following context indicates that Paul refers to the Holy Spirit. The Greek word for **put out** can be used for "extinguishing a fire" (Mark 9:48) or a lamp (Matt. 25:8). This leads John Stott to comment, "But the Holy Spirit is light as well as fire and, far from extinguishing him, we must let him both shine and burn within us."[13]

There is considerable uncertainty among interpreters as to the precise thrust of Paul's words here. Many think that he is addressing a tendency in the church to resist, in some way, the Spirit's work. And the reference to prophecies (1 Thess. 5:20) in the next clause leads many scholars to think that he has in mind the exercise of spiritual gifts in the church (see Amos 2:12; Micah 3:6).

Exactly why this admonition is necessary, we can only guess. Perhaps the leaders in the Thessalonian church, untrained and inexperienced, are unsure of themselves and, therefore, tend to suppress spontaneous contributions to worship. Their concern is understandable; certainly, such practices *can* get out of hand. Later, Paul will feel it necessary to put some restraints on the church in Corinth in connection with such activities (1 Cor. 12-14, especially 14:27-36). But here he seems to fear that the Thessalonians may move too far in the other direction. Therefore, he instructs them, **Do not treat prophecies with contempt** (1 Thess. 5:20). **Contempt** is a strong word, but so is the word in the Greek original. The older translation was "despise."

Exactly what the term **prophecies** means in this context is a difficult problem. Ernest Best notes its usages in the New Testament: "We may describe its contents as *revelation* (see 1 Cor. 14:25f.) whether this is the inauguration of a new step in the mission of the church (Acts 13:1-3), the exhortation and building up of the community (1 Cor. 14:3), the foretelling of events (Acts 11:27f.; 21:10f.), the communication of a word of the Lord (1 Thess. 4:16f.) or the disclosure of eschatological and apocalyptic information [that is, predictions concerning end-times] (the Revelation of John calls itself a 'prophecy'—1:3; 10:11, etc.)"[14]

In a different yet related line of interpretation, some scholars do not see the issue as concerning spiritual gifts as such. They think that, given the various and somewhat confused notions in the church concerning Christ's return, some may have been engaging in wild speculations and inappropriate actions with respect to the Second Coming (2 Thess. 2:2). In reaction to this, others may have swung too far the other way, shutting off all consideration of the topic.

Whatever the precise cause of the problem in Thessalonica, Paul strikes a balance in language which is still applicable to the various situations churches may face even today. He neither chokes off all spontaneous participation nor leaves the door wide open for anything and everything. **Test everything** (1 Thess. 5:21), he says, and this seems to apply not only to supposed prophecies, but literally to "*all* things." In this context, he probably has in mind particularly all aspects of congregational worship. Such testing is (perhaps even today) necessary because strange things can happen, even in churches. Elsewhere Paul mentions, apparently as an extreme example, no one speaking in the Spirit could say, "Jesus be cursed" (1 Cor. 12:3).

No criteria for evaluation are spelled out here in 1 Thessalonians, but Paul elsewhere mentions good order (1 Cor. 14:33, 40), intelligibility (14:19), and capacity to build up the church (14:3, 4, 5, etc.). John's First Epistle makes harmony with the doctrine of the Incarnation (Jesus was both God and man[15]) a test (1 John 4:1-3). The *Didache* calls for consistency in the personal life of the would-be prophet (11.10).[16] Jesus does the same: "By their fruit you will recognize them" (Matt. 7:16).

Presumably for us today the first test would involve applying relevant Scriptures (Acts 17:11; see Deuteronomy 13). Anything contrary to gospel principles is to be rejected, of course (Gal. 1:6-9). Another basic question is, "What view of Jesus Christ is being presented?" We need also to be familiar with the accepted Christian teachings held by the church, and to test with special care anything which professes to be new.

But then, after testing, the instruction is, **Hold on to the good** (1 Thess. 5:21b). The word is a strong one, meaning latch on to it and hold it fast! This requires openness to new truth and readiness to incorporate it in our thinking and living, appropriating valid insights and living by them. That is to say, we are not to become professional critics, forever testing, always holding back, never committing ourselves.

On the other hand, after testing, **Avoid every kind of evil** (5:22). This word, too, is a strong one (same Greek word as in 4:3). The call is for discernment: **test,** and then **hold on** or **avoid,** as appropriate for those bearing the name of Christ. I. Howard Marshall suggests an appropriate current application of this paragraph: "The charismatic revival has merely underlined the importance of Paul's advice here. On the one hand, it has stressed the importance of openness to the workings of the Spirit, and the renewed vigor which has come into the church shows that it is unhelpful for the church to quench the Spirit. On the other hand, the need to be discerning with regard to activities attributed to the Spirit is all the greater."[17]

3. PRAYER FOR SANCTIFICATION 5:23-24

This prayer could well be considered part of the letter's conclusion, but there is even also closer connection with what has preceded. A number of interpreters have noted that this prayer brings the second main division of the letter to a close in a manner parallel to the way in which the prayer in 3:11-13 closes the first main division. The concern at the heart of both prayers is essentially the same: the sanctification of the Thessalonian Christians, with the goal of their being found blameless and holy at the coming of Christ. Also, the prayer in 3:11-13 leads into the section which calls for holiness of life, there defined primarily in terms of sexual purity, brotherly love, and Christian community (4:1-12).

In this second main division of the letter, a high standard of expectation has been set for the Thessalonian Christians. They are called "sons of the light," and "sons of the day" (5:5). Such a description calls for the highest level of Christian living, both individually and collectively. Therefore, what is expected of them has been set forth in extreme language here: for example, "nobody," "always," "everyone" (5:15); "always," "continually," "in all circumstances" (5:16-18);

"everything" (5:21); and "every kind" (5:22). Such a level of spiritual achievement is more than the Thessalonian Christians (or anyone else) could be expected to attain through their own spiritual resources. Therefore, Paul prays that **God himself** will **sanctify [them] through and through** in order that their whole being may **be kept blameless** and be found to be so **at the coming of our Lord Jesus Christ** (5:23). Thus, the high standards of verses 12 through 22 are matched by the radical content of the prayer. Let's look at it more closely.

There is a kind of double emphasis in the prayer's address—first, **God himself** (5:23), which Leon Morris thinks reinforces the point Paul has just been making: "It is only in God that the Thessalonians will be able to do what they have been asked."[18] Then, God is further described as **the God of peace** (5:23). Paul frequently uses this characterization of God in expressions of prayer or aspiration toward the end of his letters (for example, Romans 15:33; 16:20; 2 Corinthians 13:11; Philippians 4:9; see 2 Thessalonians 3:16; Ephesians 6:23).

To understand the thrust of this, we must remember that **peace** in Scripture is more than absence of conflict and more than personal inward tranquility. Its use in the New Testament continues the concept of *shalom* in the Old Testament, with connotations of health, well-being, wholeness, even salvation. And these are understood, not individualistically, but communally. These are the marks of the kingdom of God.

This **peace** is the gift of God for His people, through His Messiah, and often associated with God's final deliverance of His people (see Numbers 6:24-26; Psalm 29:11; Isaiah 54:10; 55:12; 57:18-19; Jeremiah 33:6-9; see Luke 1:79; John 14:27; Acts 10:36; Ephesians 2:14-18). Therefore, in a prayer for the total cleansing, for the wholeness and spiritual health of the people of God in Thessalonica, it is appropriate to appeal to **the God of *peace*** (my emphasis). This is especially the case in a prayer which concludes by referring to the appearance of their coming King.

Earlier in this letter Paul prayed that through God's strengthening of their hearts, the Thessalonian Christians might become "unblamable in holiness" (3:13 Revised Standard Version). And he described their sanctification as "God's will" (4:3). It is their duty, and therefore he urges it upon them; but at the same time it can be accomplished only by the work of God in their lives, and therefore now he prays again that God will complete the process of sanctification in their lives.

Sanctification is a major concept in Christian life and thought, of course. What is involved can be illuminated by the usage of the term "sanctify" in the Old Testament. The leading idea there was the setting apart of something for God's exclusive use, separating it from ordinary human use in order to devote it to sacred purposes. This idea could be applied to a particular day of the week (the Sabbath; see Genesis 2:3); a structure (the tent and altar; see Exodus 29:43-44); or persons (Aaron and his sons for priesthood; see Exodus 30:30; also Jeremiah 1:5).

There is the negative aspect—separated *from,* and thus no longer available for ordinary human purposes, not to mention for evil purposes. And there is also the positive aspect—separated *to,* and thus fully available to God for His exclusive service. Certain items could be sanctified by placing them on the altar as an offering to God, and just by virtue of their being placed on the altar they became God's and, therefore, were considered holy (Exod. 29:37). In this case, too, "holy" would mean belonging to God, and belonging in such a way that it would be sacrilege for anyone to remove it from the altar and appropriate it for himself.

Further, in the case of *persons* set apart for God, such as priests, or indeed all Israel, sanctification involves their whole inner being. They are called to turn their external (or objective) *relationship* to God (as set apart for Him) into inward (or subjective) *resemblance,* as in Leviticus: *"Be* holy because I, the LORD your God, am holy" (Lev. 19:2, my emphasis). Unlike material objects (for example, the ark of the covenant), for *persons,* holiness becomes a matter of character and conduct. For example, the rest of Leviticus 19 lays out a series of primarily ethical requirements, frequently reinforced by "I am the LORD your God."

The principle that what is placed on the altar is thereby turned over to God for His exclusive use is applied to persons in the New Testament, as in Romans 12:1, where Christians who thus offer themselves to God are called: *"holy* and pleasing to God" (my emphasis). In principle, this applies to all God's people; therefore, in the New Testament, Christians are regularly called "saints." This means "holy ones," of course; the term is another member of the same word group with "sanctify." Alfred Plummer points to some of the implications of "saints" as a name for Christians: "To each individual Christian, therefore, the name is at once an honour, an exhortation, and a reproach. It tells him of his high calling, it exhorts him to live up to it, and it reminds him of his grievous shortcomings."[19]

So Christians are called to be "holy"; but, ultimately, fallen human beings cannot make themselves holy any more than they can lift themselves by their own bootstraps. James Denney puts this in a practical, plain and personal way: "Who has not tried to overcome a fault, to work off a vicious temper, to break for good with an evil habit, or in some other direction to sanctify himself, and withal to keep out of God's sight till the work was done? It is of no use. Only the God of Christian peace, the God of the gospel, can sanctify us; or to look at the same thing from our own side, we cannot be sanctified until we are at peace with God."[20]

Therefore, here in 1 Thessalonians 5:23, Paul is praying that God may carry the process of sanctification through to its goal; the reference to the return of Christ makes it clear that the completion of the process is in view. I. Howard Marshall says, "Here he is praying for the continuation and completion of the process. Just as Paul can refer to believers as saints or holy ones, despite their lack of actual holiness in conduct, so those who have been sanctified or set apart as God's people must increasingly show the appropriate characteristics in goodness and dedication to God's service, and Paul prays that God will work in the lives of his readers to this end."[21]

Through and through and **whole** emphasize the totality of the process Paul envisions (5:23). Taken together, they signify "in each and every part" and "in totality," resulting in completeness. That every aspect of their being is included in the scope of the prayer is further emphasized by **spirit, soul and body.** There is a scholarly consensus today that Paul does not intend by these words to offer an analysis of human nature, or to define a person as the sum total of these three aspects of his being.

The language here is parallel to that used by Jesus: "Love the Lord your God with all your heart and with all your soul and with all your mind and with all your strength" (Mark 12:30). No one thinks that Jesus intended to indicate four distinct components of human nature; rather, He is calling for *wholehearted devotion to God.* The emphasis there is on *totality.* Similarly here, Paul heaps up terms to emphasize once more the *completeness* of the transformation for which he prays, affecting every aspect of their being: spirit (1 Cor. 14:15); soul (Luke 1:46); and body (1 Cor. 6:20).

The precise connotation of **blameless** (1 Thess. 5:23) is somewhat difficult because the word is used in the New Testament only sparingly. It certainly means, at least, free from anything which would mar wholeness and integrity. Perhaps there is an echo of the requirement of Old Testament times that whatever was to be offered to God was to be without blemish or defect (Lev. 1:3). The prayer reaches forward to the Second Coming (**at the coming of our Lord Jesus Christ** [1 Thess. 5:23]) because only then will the process of sanctification be completed, and only then will all things be judged (the Judgment is implied by

blameless). A. L. Moore says, "It is then that the Christian will be seen for what he is and his works revealed in their true light (see Matt[hew] 25:31-46)."[22]

This awesome prayer—all-inclusive in breadth, and breathtaking in height—fails to stagger our imagination only because, in our Wesleyan tradition, we have heard the language so often that it has tended to lose its vividness. Perhaps we need to hear it again, fresh and challenging, for it is based upon a recurrent biblical theme: "Be holy because I, the Lord your God, am holy" (see 1 Peter 1:15-16). When we *really* hear it, then we will need, as the Thessalonian converts did, the reassurance of the promise, **The one who calls you is faithful and he will do it** (1 Thess. 5:24).

It is significant that the form of the verb **calls** implies an ongoing, persistent command and invitation, just as, for example, God called and repeatedly re-called Israel to this standard (see comments on 2:12). According to Romans 8:28-30, God's purpose for those He has *called* is for them "to be conformed to the likeness of his Son, that he might be the firstborn among many brothers" (8:29). God's house is being prepared (John 14:2-3) that it may be filled with a whole family of living likenesses to the Elder Brother. The process of being made like Him is called, in the Bible, "sanctification." And it is God's will for all His people (1 Thess. 4:3).

The confirming guarantee—**The one who calls you is faithful and he will do it** (5:24)—is stronger in the Greek text than the New International Version's **and he will do it** indicates. As Leon Morris points out, in the Greek there is an "also," but there is no "it." The omission of "it" focuses attention on the verb, "do." And the "also" indicates that God not only calls; He also acts. The Caller is also a Doer.[23] (On God's faithfulness, see 2 Thessalonians 3:3; 1 Corinthians 1:9; 10:13; 2 Corinthians 1:18; 2 Timothy 2:13; and in the Old Testament see Deuteronomy 7:9; Isaiah 49:7.) God's faithfulness to us in Christ calls for—and will provide, if we yield to Him—an answering faithfulness on our part (see Philippians 2:12-13; also 1:6).

ADDITIONAL NOTE ON SANCTIFICATION

The discussion of sanctification in the comments on 1 Thessalonians 5:23-24 dealt primarily with biblical texts. The purpose of this additional note is to call attention to more theological and experiential aspects of sanctification. The discussion will be simple, perhaps simplistic. It is cheerfully acknowledged that it will be regarded as traditional.

The first effort will be to locate sanctification in the context of Christian experience. Where does sanctification fit among the usually recognized stages in the Christian's spiritual journey? It must be acknowledged "right up front" that the stages listed are inevitably somewhat artificial. Theologians attempt to detect and classify the basic elements of Christian experience and to understand their inter-relationship. They provide a framework for thinking systematically about these matters. But, of course, few Christians consciously move from one to the next of these stages, checking them off one by one as they make their own spiritual journey.

1. CALLING: The initiative in Christian experience lies not in ourselves, but in the call of God. Wesleyans believe in what theologians call "prevenient grace," the grace that is at work in our lives before we come to know Him. We seek Him because He first sought us. The lifted-up Christ draws all people toward himself (see John 12:32).

2. CONVERSION: The Christian's initial response to God's gracious initiative includes two aspects: (a) *repentance* (see Matthew 4:17)—turning from sin, acknowledging guilt and selfishness; a change of mind leading to a change of conduct; and (b) *faith* (see Romans 1:16)—turning to God, trusting Christ for forgiveness of sins.

3. JUSTIFICATION and REGENERATION: Instantaneously and simultaneously, the new Christian is (a) *justified* (see Romans 3:24; 5:1)—is pardoned of sins, acquitted in the court of heaven by grace through faith, on the basis of Christ's atonement for sin; a judicial act of God; and (b) *regenerated* (see John 3:7)—is born again (or adopted; see Romans 8:23; Ephesians 1:5) into the family of God, experiences newness of life inwardly through the indwelling of Christ by His Spirit; a creative act of God.

4. SANCTIFICATION: Beginning in that same moment is the lifelong process of *sanctification,* growth in personal holiness (more fully treated below).

5. GLORIFICATION: This is the goal of the sanctification process, the consummation of our Christian experience; at the return of Christ, an instantaneous transformation "in the twinkling of an eye" (see 1 Corinthians 15:52), when "we shall be like him, for we shall see him as he is" (see 1 John 3:2).

This survey of stages in the Christian life provides the setting for further consideration of sanctification. The word itself, *sanctification* (or *holiness*) translates three Greek nouns, all of which are derived from the same root word. According to a doctoral dissertation by Dr. Claude Ries, the words are *hagiasmos*—sanctification as a process (see Romans 6:19, 22; 1 Corinthians 1:30; 1 Thessalonians 4:3-4, 7; 2 Thessalonians 2:13; 1 Timothy 2:15; Hebrews 12:14; 1 Peter 1:2); *hagiosune*—sanctification as the goal, the result of the process; holiness, purity (Rom. 1:4; 1 Thess. 3:13; 2 Cor. 7:1); and *hagiotes*—holiness "as an abstract quality" (Ries); moral purity (2 Cor. 1:12; Heb. 12:10).[24]

The use of the first two terms in 1 Thessalonians illustrates the differences just indicated: 4:3-4, 7 refer to sanctification as a process; and 3:13, to sanctification as a goal or result. (In 5:23, the verb from the same Greek root is used to ask God to carry the process through to its consummation at the return of Christ.) As stated in the comments on 5:23, the basic idea of sanctification includes two aspects: (1) set apart *from,* indicating cleansing, purification, getting rid of hindrances to serving God; and (2) set apart *to,* fully turned over to God for His use, all placed on the "altar" and thus surrendered to Him.

Theologians distinguish between *initial* and *progressive* sanctification. The former recognizes that, according to the New Testament, *all* Christians are indwelt by the Holy Spirit (see Romans 8:9; Galatians 4:6). They are regularly called "saints" (Rom. 1:7) or "sanctified" (1 Cor. 1:2); they are "in Christ," and thus set apart to God. *Progressive* sanctification is the ongoing work of the Holy Spirit. As their spiritual journey progresses, Christians become more sensitive to sin in their lives, turn to God for deliverance, and thus continue to grow in grace.

The Wesleyan Church also speaks of *entire* sanctification, a major turning point ("second definite work of grace"), in which the Christian, in a deliberate act of total surrender, seeks the fullness of the Holy Spirit (to be not just "indwelt," but "infilled"). It is recognized that, even after major turning points in one's Christian pilgrimage (whether "second" or however many), the new commitment will need to be reiterated day-by-day, in the light of new circumstances, with deepening understanding of the way of Christ. John Wesley taught that even "the best of men need Christ as their Priest, their Atonement, their Advocate with the Father; not only as the continuance of their every blessing depends on His death and intercession, but on account of their coming short of the law of love. For every living man does so."[25]

The topic is complex. One way to get to the heart of the issue might be to ask what, concretely, it would mean for a human being to be holy

106

in the ultimate degree, to be filled with the Spirit, as Paul prays in Ephesians 3:19, "to the measure of all the fullness of God." The answer is plain. It happened once. There once was a totally God-filled man, and His name is Jesus. To become holy is to become Christlike.

ENDNOTES

[1]F. F. Bruce, *1 and 2 Thessalonians*, Word Biblical Commentary (Waco, Texas: Word Books, Publisher, 1982), p. 119.

[2]Leon Morris, *The First and Second Epistles to the Thessalonians,* rev. ed., New International Commentary on the New Testament (Grand Rapids, Michigan: Wm. B. Eerdmans Publishing Co., 1991), p. 167.

[3]I. Howard Marshall, *1 and 2 Thessalonians,* New Century Bible Commentary (Grand Rapids, Michigan: Wm. B. Eerdmans Publishing Co., 1983), p. 150.

[4]Charles A. Wanamaker, *The Epistles to the Thessalonians*, New International Greek Testament Commentary (Grand Rapids, Michigan: Wm. B. Eerdmans Publishing Co., 1990), p. 198.

[5]James Denney, *The Epistles to the Thessalonians,* Expositor's Bible (New York: George H. Doran Co., n.d.), p. 212.

[6]John Stott, *The Gospel and the End of Time* (Downers Grove, Illinois: InterVarsity Press, 1991), pp. 122–23.

[7]Bruce, p. 126.

[8]Morris, p. 172n.

[9]Morris, p. 173.

[10]Stott, p. 125.

[11]The Gospels include the New Testament books of Matthew, Mark, Luke, and John.

[12]John Wesley, *Explanatory Notes upon the New Testament* (London: Epworth Press, 1950), p. 762.

[13]Stott, p. 131.

[14]Ernest Best, *A Commentary on the First and Second Epistles to the Thessalonians*, Harper's New Testament Commentaries (New York: Harper and Row Publishers, 1972), p. 239.

[15]The Incarnation was God's coming to us in the person of Jesus.

[16]The *Didache* is an early Christian writing, written about A.D. 112.

[17]Marshall, p. 160.

[18]Morris, p. 180.

[19]Alfred Plummer, *St. James and St. Jude,* Expositor's Bible (London: Hodder and Stoughton, 1891), p. 379.

[20]Denney, p. 252.

[21]Marshall, p. 161.

[22]A. L. Moore, *1 and 2 Thessalonians,* Century Bible (London: Thomas Nelson and Sons, Ltd., 1969), p. 87.

[23]Morris, p. 184.

Present: Congregational Duties

[24]Claude A. Ries, "A Greek New Testament Approach to the Teaching of the Deeper Spiritual Life" (Ph.D. diss., Northern Baptist Theological Seminary, 1945), pp. 57–81, *passim.*

[25]John Wesley, *A Plain Account of Christian Perfection* (London: Epworth Press, 1952), p. 73.

6

CONCLUSION
1 Thessalonians 5:25-28

Following generally the contemporary pattern for ending letters, Paul now quickly moves to bring this letter to a close. He makes three requests, two of them common to most of his letters, one less usual, and then blesses them with a standard (but not merely mechanical) benediction.

1. CLOSING EXHORTATIONS 5:25-27

Paul's request to the Thessalonians, **Brothers, pray for us** (1 Thess. 5:25), is a frequent request in his letters (see, for example, 2 Thessalonians 3:1-2; Romans 15:30-32; Colossians 4:3; also Ephesians 6:18-20; Philippians 1:19; Philemon 22). He has just prayed for them, and now he asks them to reciprocate. The form of the verb indicates that he is asking them to pray regularly for him and for his apostolic team (**us** [1 Thess. 5:25]). Paul believed in the value of mutual intercession. He thought it made the crucial difference—at both ends, so to speak, those prayed for and those praying (Phil. 1:3-8, 19).

Greet all the brothers with a holy kiss (1 Thess. 5:26) is a stronger than usual expression (but see Romans 16:16; 1 Corinthians 16:20; 2 Corinthians 13:12). More often the instruction was simply to greet one another. The kiss was an accepted form of affectionate greeting, without sexual connotation, within the family (**brothers**), and the addition of **holy** marks this out as a *Christian* relationship (1 Thess. 5:26). J. B. Phillips' rendition, "Give a handshake all round among the brotherhood" (1 Thess. 5:26, *The New Testament in Modern English*) perhaps over-modernizes the instruction; but one way or another, when they gather, Christians ought to express mutual affection in the culturally appropriate manner.

Verse 27 has several unexpected features: (1) The singular **I** is surprising, after "we" and "us" through most of the letter; perhaps it simply means Paul is taking over the pen from the person who had been transcribing the letter (see 2 Thessalonians 3:17; 1 Corinthians 16:21; Galatians 6:11; Colossians 4:18); (2) the word **charge** is a strong expression, especially when reinforced with **before the Lord;** it indicates real earnestness on Paul's part; and (3) some have interpreted the **all** as indicating division in the congregation (Paul had just used the word in the preceding sentence), but there is no indication elsewhere in the letter; surely Paul would have addressed the problem more directly than this—it is more likely that he feared the sort of situation indicated by 2 Thessalonians 2:1-2.

We may note in passing that **read** means "read aloud" (1 Thess. 5:27); many in the congregation would be illiterate. We may have a more accurate picture of the actual situation if we remember that, for the most part, the early Christians met in small, separate house-churches. Thus, on a given Lord's Day, the Thessalonian Christians would be meeting in several places, and the various gatherings were probably marked by geographical, ethnic, linguistic, and socioeconomic distinctives (for example, merchants in the Jewish quarter here, Greek-speaking slaves there, leather workers elsewhere). Paul wants to make sure that every sub-group receives this communication. His concern includes them **all** (5:27).

2. BENEDICTION 5:28

Paul's final words in this first Letter to the Thessalonians, **The grace of our Lord Jesus Christ be with you,** is more or less Paul's standard benedictory prayer (1 Thess. 5:28; see Romans 16:20b; 1 Corinthians 16:23). It states what was basic in early Christian thinking—that Jesus Christ is the mediator of the grace of God which initiated and carried through to completion their salvation (see 1 Thessalonians 5:24; Philippians 1:6). Therefore, they acknowledge Christ as *Lord.*

2 THESSALONIANS OUTLINE

I. ENCOURAGEMENT (1:1-12)
  A. Address (1:1-2)
  B. Thanksgiving for the Thessalonians' Growth (1:3-4)
  C. Promise of Vindication (1:5-10)
  D. Prayer for Fulfillment of Calling (1:11-12)

II. EXPLANATION (2:1-17)
  A. The Need for Explanation (2:1-2)
  B. The Man of Lawlessness (2:3-12)
    1. 2:3-4   His Coming and Character
    2. 2:5-7   His Present Restraining
    3. 2:8-12   His Revelation and Destruction
  C. Assurance of Salvation (2:13-17)
    1. 2:13-14   Paul Gives Thanks for Them
    2. 2:15   Paul Exhorts Them
    3. 2:16-17   Paul Prays for Them

III. EXHORTATION (3:1-18)
  A. Mutual Concern Expressed (3:1-5)
    1. 3:1-2   Request for Prayer
    2. 3:3-5   Assurance for the Thessalonians
  B. Instruction Concerning the Idle (3:6-15)
    1. 3:6   Keep Away
    2. 3:7-9   Paul's Example
    3. 3:10   Paul's Command
    4. 3:11-15   Instruction to the Congregation
  C. Conclusion (3:16-18)
    1. 3:16   Prayer for Peace
    2. 3:17   Final Greeting
    3. 3:18   Benediction

Part Three

ENCOURAGEMENT

2 Thessalonians 1:1-12

Second Thessalonians begins with a fairly standard Pauline greeting (2 Thess. 1:1-2) and expression of thanksgiving (1:3-4). But then, after that, as I. Howard Marshall observes, the pattern of thought resembles that of the first letter: There, in 1 Thess. 1:4, Paul "slides over" from thanksgiving to the story of how the Thessalonians first became Christians; here, in verse 5, he slides over from thanksgiving for their perseverance in faith to encouragement by means of a promise of vindication at the return of Christ. And in both cases, he makes these shifts without a noticeable break in the progression of thought.[1]

Here, on the basis of the central affirmation that **God is just** (1:6), Paul assures the Thessalonians that their faithfulness will not go unnoticed and unrewarded (1:5-10). When the Lord Jesus returns in power and glory, the persecutors of His people will be punished for their rejection of the gospel by exclusion from His presence, while His holy people will participate in the glory of that day.

The final note of encouragement in this section is Paul's assurance of his unceasing prayer on their behalf: that God would count them worthy of His call to the kingdom of God, and empower them to practice in their daily lives the implications of their faith, to the glory of their Lord (1:11-12).

ENDNOTE

[1]I. Howard Marshall, *1 and 2 Thessalonians,* New Century Bible Commentary (Grand Rapids, Michigan: Wm. B. Eerdmans Publishing Co., 1983), p. 169.

7

ADDRESS

2 Thessalonians 1:1-2

We need not say much about Paul's address, for it is almost identical with its parallel in 1 Thessalonians: same writers, same readers, virtually the same greeting (see comments on 1 Thessalonians 1:1). There are two small, but not insignificant, differences from the address in the first letter: (1) **our** is added to **Father,** indicating that Paul has in mind God's fatherhood with respect to the Thessalonians rather than with respect to Christ; and (2) the Source of **grace and peace** is spelled out—**from God the Father** (no "our" this time) **and the Lord Jesus Christ** (2 Thess. 2:1-2). This becomes Paul's usual custom in later letters (see Romans 1:7; 1 Corinthians 1:3; 2 Corinthians 1:2; Ephesians 1:2; Philippians 1:2; Colossians 1:2; Philemon 3).

Thus, the simple addition of **our** to **Father** adds a reassuring note, and contributes to the encouragement which is the primary purpose of the first division of this letter. Perhaps Paul also intends **our** to provide further comfort for the Thessalonian Christians by reminding them that they and their missionaries are members of the same family of God, along with other congregations everywhere (2 Thess. 1:4).

Once again **Father** and Son (**Lord Jesus Christ**) are set side-by-side with a single preposition, **from,** in a manner which is in harmony with—if not proof of—their oneness in nature and work. This seems commonplace to us, but it is remarkable language for one like Paul (trained in Judaism[1]) with its basic affirmation: "The Lord our God is one." Leon Morris quotes G. B. Wilson: "That such a construction could be used without comment not only implies the writer's belief in the deity of Christ, but also takes the readers' acknowledgment of it for granted."[2]

ENDNOTES

[1]Judaism is the life and belief system of the Jewish people and involves a covenant relationship with God. Though there are various branches of Judaism,

115

the underlying theme among them is monotheism and a recognition of the Law, or the Torah (the first five books of the Old Testament: Genesis, Exodus, Leviticus, Numbers, and Deuteronomy).

[2]Leon Morris, *The First and Second Epistles to the Thessalonians,* rev. ed., New International Commentary on the New Testament (Grand Rapids, Michigan: Wm. B. Eerdmans Publishing Co., 1991), p. 192.

THANKSGIVING FOR THE THESSALONIANS' GROWTH

2 Thessalonians 1:3-4

In most of the letters of Paul which have been preserved for us, the opening greeting is immediately followed by a thanksgiving. What is unique here in 2 Thessalonians 1 is that he seems to describe this thankfulness as an *obligation;* **ought** is reinforced by **and rightly so** (2 Thess. 1:3). The New Revised Standard Version translates this, "We must always give thanks . . . as is right." Some interpreters have read this as demonstrating a certain coldness or formality, a sense of dutifulness. But nothing in the immediate context indicates that the gratitude is expressed grudgingly. In fact, the words which follow are warm and enthusiastic.

It is, of course, *right* that the missionaries should give thanks to God for what has been happening among the Thessalonian converts. They have yet much to learn; this letter will seek to correct some significant deficiencies in theological understanding and lapses in conduct. But, in spite of all that, Paul and his colleagues are clear-sighted enough to recognize and appreciate their strengths, rather than just focusing on their flaws. And, in accordance with sound pastoral practice, they will mention these first, before dealing with problems.

But there is more than good psychology at work here. Paul is genuinely grateful to God for significant progress by the Thessalonian

Christians in fundamental aspects of authentic Christian living. On the one hand, their **faith is growing more and more** (1:3). In the original Greek, the word for **growing** is a strong one, and the form of the verb indicates that it is an ongoing process. Their faith is flourishing. Therefore, Paul is motivated to give thanks because, before this, precisely their faith had been a point of concern for their missionaries, as expressed in 1 Thessalonians 3:2, 5, 7, and especially, verse 10.

And, again, the Thessalonians' **love . . . is increasing** (2 Thess. 1:3). Once more, the verb is a strong word, often translated *abounding*. The form of the verb shows continuation, and this is reinforced by **every one of you . . . for each other** (1:3, "each for all and all for each" [New English Bible]). For this, too, the missionaries had prayed (1 Thess. 3:12) and exhorted (4:10). No wonder, then, that they feel the need to be grateful to God; He is answering their prayers!

In consequence (**therefore** [2 Thess. 1:4]) Paul holds them up as a model for other churches (compare 1 Thessalonians 1:7), particularly for their **perseverance,** their endurance and steadfastness; and for their **faith,** their consistent life of trustfulness in God—perhaps one could say, their faith becoming faithfulness (the same Greek word can mean both).

And this is taking place in spite of **all the persecutions and trials** they **are enduring** (2 Thess. 1:4). David Williams distinguishes these two terms: "The more general word 'trials' . . . means 'pressures' and can refer to any of the pressures to which we as human beings are subject in 'this present evil age' (Gal[atians] 1:4). 'Persecutions' is more specific. . . . and refers in particular to trials that come to us as Christians. . . ."[1] These are trials that are caused by, for instance, our faith in Christ. The Thessalonian Christians' tribulations are numerous, varied, and ongoing, but they are continuing to make progress in basic elements of Christian living, such as **faith** and **love**. (Hope, the third member of the common triad [1 Thess. 1:3; 5:8] is not explicitly mentioned here. Some interpreters think that hope is *implied* by the Thessalonians' perseverance; they persist because they anticipate a better future.)

Thus far, then, Paul has provided encouragement: (1) by telling the Thessalonians of his gratitude to God for their progress, even under adverse circumstances; and (2) by mentioning his fatherly pride in them, openly expressed to the congregations (**God's churches** [2 Thess. 1:4]) he has been visiting or writing (for example, 2 Corinthians 8:1-5—from a later period). But now he proceeds to provide further motivation for the steadfastness in Christian commitment they will need in a world which is no friend to grace.

ENDNOTE

[1]David Williams, *1 and 2 Thessalonians,* New International Bible Commentary (Peabody, Massachusetts: Hendrikson Publishers, 1992), p. 112.

9

PROMISE
OF VINDICATION

2 Thessalonians 1:5-10

T he precise connection between this section and the opening
paragraph is not entirely clear. Actually, 2 Thessalonians 1:3-10
translates one long sentence in the Greek original, but readable
English requires a new beginning here. The precise thrust of **all this** (1:5)
is not obvious. Perhaps it takes in all that immediately precedes, and
expands on the *significance* of their perseverance and faith under ongoing
persecutions and trials, for which he had just thanked God. In that case,
it would be understood to mean that their perseverance and faith in the
midst of trials is evidence, somehow, of God's rightful judgment.

This interpretation appears to be confirmed by the parallel in
Philippians 1:28, where the word translated "sign" has the same Greek
root as that translated "evidence" here. In that passage, the courage and
faith which the Philippian Christians displayed in their united stand for
the gospel was a "sign" of the ultimate destruction of their enemies, and
of their own salvation. This will be God's doing. But in the meantime
God "grants" them (that is, bestows as a favor) the privilege of suffering
for Christ (Phil. 1:27b-30).

Similarly, here in the Thessalonian passage, these Christians' faith is
sustaining them even under persecution, and Paul is encouraging their
confidence in God. After all, **God is just** (2 Thess. 1:6), and thus His
judgment is right (1:5). Therefore, all that they are presently
undergoing will, in the end, work for their ultimate blessing: they **will be
counted worthy of the kingdom of God** (1:5) at the return of Christ,
when everything will be sorted out.

Paul's intention, then, is to strengthen and comfort and encourage the
Thessalonian converts by providing a glimpse of the End (1:5-10). The

passage may serve also to prepare the way for the more detailed description of selected final events in the next section of the letter (2:1-12). But first, we need to look more closely at the sometimes difficult details of the passage before us.

It is implied that the Thessalonian Christians are seeking participation in **the kingdom of God** (1:5). This Kingdom played a major role in the teaching of Jesus, especially as reported in the first three Gospels.¹ The concept is less prominent in the teaching of Paul. Occasionally he refers to it as a present reality (for example, Romans 14:17), but more often the term designates the future community of God's redeemed people at the second coming of Christ, as it obviously does here (see 1 Corinthians 6:9; 15:24; Galatians 5:21; 2 Timothy 4:1). Both Jesus and Paul consistently make a close connection between the Kingdom and suffering (for example, Matthew 5:10-12; Luke 6:20-23; Acts 14:22; Romans 8:17; 2 Timothy 2:11-12).

Paul explicitly makes a connection here: **kingdom of God, for which you are suffering** (2 Thess. 1:5). The connection is close, but not *direct*. It is not suffering *in order to gain,* but rather *on behalf of which* **you are suffering.** They must not rely on their sufferings to *earn* them a place in the Kingdom; then they would always be haunted by the question, "Has this been enough?" Rather, their confidence rests on the character of God: **God's judgment is right** because **God is just** (1:5-6). Ernest Best explains, "The persecuted will have peace and the persecutors will be punished—because God is righteous. In the final issue this results from the nature of God and not from their achievement," and then he clinches the matter by adding, "any other result would entail an immoral universe."²

Verses 7 through 10, then, expand on the consequences of this fundamental principle for the Thessalonians and their persecutors. In capsule form, it means: **trouble to those who trouble** (1:6) and **relief to you who are troubled** (1:7). This is not in the spirit of retaliation; it is the recognition that in a moral universe the consequences of evil cannot be the same as those for righteousness. Our confidence that this is true is not based on some abstract philosophical principle, but is founded on the righteous nature of God. And He is the God who acts in history, who controls the destiny of all humankind—and therefore, of course, the future of the Thessalonian Christians.

And Paul immediately includes himself and his colleagues: **and to us as well** (1:7). This is perhaps intended to comfort the Thessalonians by reminding them that he is not writing this from an ivory tower somewhere;

their missionaries experience the same tribulation and share the same hope as they do. In fact, Paul says, *all* Christians share in this, to some degree, at least (see 1 Thessalonians 3:3-4; Acts 14:22). What is here promised the Thessalonians initially might seem minimal and mainly negative in nature—**relief** (1:7; in several other versions, "rest"). The word was used for loosening a taut bowstring, and thus suggests release from tension, relaxation of pressure. For someone who has been stretched to capacity for some time, that might seem a very great blessing indeed.

The central figure in the coming revelation is, of course, **the Lord Jesus** (2 Thess. 1:7), and three phrases describe significant features which distinguish this manifestation from that of the "gentle and humble" Jesus of His first coming (see Matthew 11:29). First, He appears **from heaven,** which suggests that He comes from God and, therefore, with authority to execute judgment (2 Thess. 1:7). Second, He appears in **blazing fire.** Fire often marked divine self-manifestations (for example, Exodus 3:2; 19:18; 24:17; see Revelation 1:14) and occasions of divine judgment (see Isaiah 30:27-30; 66:15; Daniel 7:9). Actually, the wording here in the Greek is, literally, "fire of flame," which suggests fire in motion, emphasizing the notion of judgment (see 2 Peter 3:7, 10; 1 Corinthians 3:13-15). Third, He appears accompanied by an entourage of **his powerful angels;** this reinforces the portrayal of majesty, power, and glory (see Mark 8:38; Luke 12:8-9; Matthew 24:31—angels gather the elect; Matt. 13:41, 49—angels separate out the wicked).

Two rather subtle but significant details of translation may be mentioned here: (1) Many scholars think that **his powerful angels** should be rendered "angels of *his* power," which would mean that they do not act on their own authority but at His command as agents of His power; and (2) the sequence of words in the Greek text has "in blazing fire" *after* "his powerful angels," which, thus, may be read as leading into the next clause and therefore connected with **punish** (1:8). The New Revised Standard Version has for verse 8, "in flaming fire, inflicting vengeance." Obviously, neither of these alternative translations seriously affects the total picture.

The rest of the paragraph, verses 8 through 10, pictures the radically different destinies—on the one hand, of the persecutors, and on the other, of those persecuted for the Kingdom's sake—when the Lord Jesus is revealed from heaven. He comes to punish the disobedient and to share His glory with those who belong to Him.

The passage here uses pictorial language of the kind common to contemporary Jewish end-time representations. It is difficult to distinguish which features are literal and which figurative. Leon Morris cites William Neil concerning the restraint Paul shows: "The most noticeable feature is the reticence of the description. What in normal apocalyptic [end-time] literature would have included a lurid picture of the tortures of the damned and the bliss of the righteous, in Paul's hands becomes a restrained background of Judgment with the light focused on the Person of Christ as Judge."[3] Interpreters will differ on the meaning of various details in this picture, but this much is certain: it bears witness to terrible and glorious realities in which we all will one day find ourselves involved, on the one side or the other. The meaning is clear enough to serve as severe warning and powerful encouragement.

This finale will occur in connection with the second coming of Christ, when He is **revealed** (1:7). **Revealed** will be a key word in 2:3-12. The word places less emphasis on the *coming* of Christ as such, and rather focuses on the disclosure of that which, until then, has been hidden from view.

Verses 8 and 9 of 2 Thessalonians 1 further describe the negative side of the judgment picture here. It is important to recognize that the punishment mentioned here is not vindictive or capricious. As George Findlay expresses it, "it is the inflicting of *full justice* on the criminal—nothing more, nothing less."[4] This idea of equity is also indicated by **pay back** in verse 6. The principle is, "A man reaps what he sows" (see Galatians 6:7). Otherwise, God would not be **just,** nor his **judgment right** (2 Thess. 1:5-6).

Interpreters find it difficult to determine whether Paul contemplates two distinct groups of people or gives a double description which applies to all who are subject to **God's judgment** (1:8). **Those who do not know God** could mean Gentiles (see Jeremiah 10:25; Romans 1:18; 1 Thessalonians 4:5), and those who **do not obey the gospel** could refer to Jews who have rejected their Messiah (see Isaiah 66:4; Romans 10:3). But it is perhaps more likely that Paul provides a twofold indictment of those subject to divine judgment, both Jews and Gentiles: (1) they have turned away from God's self-revelation in nature and history (Rom. 1:18-23); and (2) have also rejected the fuller revelation through Jesus. On the other hand, perhaps Paul is not thinking of such distinctions at all. Immediately in mind as subject to divine judgment are those who have defied God by persecuting His people.

The destiny of the disobedient is **everlasting destruction** (2 Thess. 1:9). This is a difficult phrase. Charles Wanamaker comments, "As there is no evidence in Paul (or the rest of the New Testament for that matter) for a concept of final annihilation of the godless, the expression 'eternal destruction' should probably be taken as indicating the severity of the punishment awaiting the enemies of God . . . without seeking to specify its exact content beyond what Paul himself expresses in the following phrase."[5]

Thus, whatever else may be involved in the punishment of the disobedient, here Paul focuses on their deprivation. Forever they will be excluded from **the presence of the Lord** (1:9; see Matthew 7:23; 8:12; 25:30), and from the overwhelming **majesty of his power.** Many think that in the background of Paul's mind here are verses like Isaiah 2:10, 19 and 21, which describe the terror on that day of those who have opposed themselves to Almighty God.

It is almost unbearably sad to think of what these will have missed. They will never experience the joy pictured in 1 Thessalonians 4:17. John Stott comments, "For the horror of this will not be so much the pain which may accompany it as the tragedy which is inherent in it, namely, that human beings made by God, like God, and for God, should spend eternity without God, irrevocably banished from his presence. . . . Instead of being fulfilled or 'glorified,' their humanity will shrink and shrivel and be destroyed. Instead of shining with the glory of Christ, their light will be extinguished in outer darkness."[6]

With verse 10, Paul turns to the positive side of the picture, to those who, rather than fleeing from the majestic and powerful presence of the Lord, will be irresistibly drawn to Him. *This* will be the glorious destiny of those who are now enduring persecution for His sake; they will not only see, but also participate in His glory. They are here identified as **his holy people** because God's sanctifying power has been transforming their lives, and as **those who have believed** because they committed themselves to Christ when the gospel came to them. Rather than being **shut out from the presence of the Lord** (1:9), they will experience what Paul later described: "When Christ, who is your life, appears, then you also will appear with him in glory" (Col. 3:4).

But when we look more closely, the picture here rather complements that of Colossians. Paul describes the Second Coming in a way which focuses attention on Christ. The saints glorify *Him,* and believers marvel at *Him!* If they "appear with Him in glory," it is to form part of the great welcoming chorus which will finally give Him the glory which is due His name. They will marvel at the wonders of His matchless grace, the grace which, at last, has brought them to their goal (Phil. 3:12-14), the goal God purposed for them from "before the creation of the world" (Eph. 1:4-5; see Romans 8:29-30). They will have been "transformed into his likeness" (2 Cor. 3:18). As F. F. Bruce has said, "nothing can so much redound to [Christ's] glory as the presentation of sinful men and women redeemed and glorified through his sacrifice on the cross."[7] In all this, they will be participating in what may fairly be called the goal of history (Phil. 2:9-11).

Paul closes the paragraph rather awkwardly in the Greek (smoothed out by the New International Version), almost interrupting himself to emphasize the point that the Thessalonian Christians will surely be included in that great throng of worshipers. They belong there because they have **believed** (2 Thess. 1:10). Paul makes sure they see themselves there, celebrating the Majestic Presence. All through this description he has been remembering the need of the Thessalonian Christians for encouragement. He wants them to lift up their heads because their redemption is drawing near (Luke 21:28)

We may note in passing that some readers have regarded this description of the Second Coming as so different from the picture in 1 Thessalonians 4:13-18 that they have doubted whether both could come from the same author. But we should remember that 1 Thessalonians focuses on what happens concerning the dead in Christ; this presents a more general picture of the glory of the returning Lord in which persecutors are punished and the faithful participate in Christ's glory.

ENDNOTES

[1]The Gospels include the New Testament books of Matthew, Mark, Luke, and John.

[2]Ernest Best, *A Commentary on the First and Second Epistles to the Thessalonians*, Harper's New Testament Commentaries (New York: Harper and Row Publishers, 1972), p. 256.

[3]Leon Morris, *The First and Second Epistles to the Thessalonians*, rev. ed., New International Commentary on the New Testament (Grand Rapids, Michigan: Wm. B. Eerdmans Publishing Co., 1991), p. 201.

[4]George G. Findlay, *The Epistles to the Thessalonians*, Cambridge Bible for Schools and Colleges (Cambridge: The University Press, 1894), p. 133.

[5]Charles A. Wanamaker, *The Epistles to the Thessalonians*, New International Greek Testament Commentary (Grand Rapids, Michigan: Wm. B. Eerdmans Publishing Co., 1990), p. 229.

[6]John Stott, *The Gospel and the End of Time* (Downers Grove, Illinois: InterVarsity Press, 1991), p. 154.

[7]F. F. Bruce, *1 and 2 Thessalonians*, Word Biblical Commentary (Waco, Texas: Word Books, Publisher, 1982), pp. 154–55.

10

PRAYER FOR FULFILLMENT OF CALLING

2 Thessalonians 1:11-12

Paul has been encouraging the Thessalonian converts (1) by expressing his gratitude to God for their growth in faith and love, and for their perseverance even under persecution; and (2) by assuring them that they will be counted worthy of participation in the glory of Christ's return. But there *is* an implied *if.* "Christian perseverance is a matter of continuing prayer and continuing faith. So Paul at last expresses how he prays that his readers will eventually reach the kingdom of God through continuing to show the evidences of living faith."[1] This assurance, too, is intended for their encouragement.

In **with this in mind** (2 Thess. 1:11; literally, "to this end") Paul gathers up what he has been saying, at least back to verse 5, and perhaps to verse 3, and carries it forward—forward into the example he provides here of the sort of prayer he offers on their behalf **constantly.** As their spiritual father (1 Thess. 2:11-12), he carries them unceasingly in his heart. This is now his second letter of instruction and encouragement, but for him, ministerial responsibility involves more than preaching and teaching (see 2 Corinthians 11:28).

We may observe also that the prayer is addressed to **our God** (2 Thess. 1:11; see 1:1). Again, with **our** Paul places himself alongside the Thessalonians, in a manner illustrative of the pastoral sensitivity he shows consistently in these letters.

A key word in the first petition here has generated complex theological debate among interpreters, as will be readily seen by consulting various English Bible versions. The point at issue is whether to translate the verb as **count you worthy** or as "make you worthy" (the debate also reaches back to verse 5, where another form of the Greek word occurs). This discussion, however, is beyond our purposes here.

I. Howard Marshall's observation seems careful and evenhanded: "In both verses it is probable that the literal meaning of the word is to deem worthy, but it is equally true that God cannot deem worthy any whom he himself has not made worthy by his action rather than by their good works; hence the force of the verb is tantamount to 'make worthy.' This is made clear by the rest of the clause. Those who God deems worthy are those in whom he can fulfill every good resolve and work of faith."[2]

It is obvious from the immediate context here (as well as from Scripture as a whole) that the worthiness required lies beyond the capability of human achievement, and therefore divine enabling is necessary. Thus Paul prays that God may **by his power . . . fulfill** (1:11). And the note of human dependence on God is reinforced by his introducing again the note of divine **calling.** D. E. Hiebert says, "The call to salvation looked forward to its consummation in the coming kingdom (1 Thess 2:12). That prospect must have a sanctifying effect on their lives now. But God must work the necessary holiness in them."[3] (See comments on "call" found in 1 Thessalonians 2:12; 4:7; 5:24; and see Ephesians 4:1).

Paul prays that, beyond their *verbal* witness for Christ, they will *live out* their Christian life as **prompted by [their] faith** (2 Thess. 1:11) not only in intention (**purpose**) but also in actual deed (**act**). He wants them to fulfill the implications of the faith they profess—in lifestyle, for example. The right response to the gospel is *obedience* (2 Thess. 1:8).

Such a pattern of witnessing by word and deed is possible, of course, only by **the grace of our God and the Lord Jesus Christ** (1:12). Compare Paul's words in his letter to the Philippians: "Continue to work out your salvation with fear and trembling, for it is God who works in you to will and to act according to his good purpose" (Phil. 2:12c-13). This exhorts believers to act because God is already acting, thus intermingling the divine and human action, but with the divine clearly previous.

The result will be **that the name of our Lord Jesus may be glorified in you, and you in him** (2 Thess. 1:12a; see 1 Peter 1:7). This points to the ultimate goal—Christ's glory and, closely connected, their own participation in it (2 Thess. 1:10). Sharing His eternal glory grows out of living for His glory now. According to F. F. Bruce, "The missionaries' prayer has the Advent in view, but it will be fulfilled in them only as their converts are progressively transformed by the Spirit here and now into the image of Christ."[4] How? **According to the grace of our God and the Lord Jesus Christ** (1:12b). Both present salvation and future glorification are traced to their ultimate source in divine grace, so that, in fact, *all* the glory belongs to Him.

Finally, it should again be noted that Paul's treatment of the second coming of Christ does not cater to satisfying curiosity, but his aim is to strengthen the call for holiness of life. The doctrine of the return of Christ appears in the New Testament primarily as a motivation for right living.

ENDNOTES

[1] I. Howard Marshall, *1 and 2 Thessalonians,* New Century Bible Commentary (Grand Rapids, Michigan: Wm. B. Eerdmans Publishing Co., 1983), p. 181.

[2] Ibid., p. 182.

[3] D. E. Hiebert, *The Thessalonian Letters* (Chicago: Moody Press, 1971), p. 296.

[4] F. F. Bruce, *1 and 2 Thessalonians,* Word Biblical Commentary (Waco, Texas: Word Books, Publisher, 1982), p. 157.

Part Four

EXPLANATION

2 Thessalonians 2:1-17

In this section of the letter we come face-to-face with one of the main reasons the letter was written. Evidently, the belief on the part of some in the Thessalonian congregation that the Day of the Lord is already present is causing confusion and anxiety. Paul refutes this notion by declaring that other events must occur first, most notably the appearance of the lawless one.

His argument is sometimes difficult to follow for at least two reasons: (1) He is reviewing highlights of more detailed teaching he gave them orally when he was among them (2 Thess. 2:5), and, of course, we do not have access to that body of teaching; and (2) because this is only a reminder, and not the initial presentation, Paul does not feel the need to develop his treatment of the topic step-by-step, systematically. He mentions the revealing of **the man of lawlessness** (2:3-4); Paul then goes back to the period before the man's appearance (2:5-7). He indicates next the man's destruction (2:8), but then describes the man's activities before that destruction (2:9-12).

Paul's practical purposes in verses 1 through 12 appear to be (1) to put a stop to the Thessalonians' alarm over the claim that the Day of the Lord had already come; (2) to prevent their being deceived by erroneous teaching concerning the last days; and, longer range, (3) to warn about the deceitful character of the campaign to be conducted by the lawless one because, for all Paul knows, they might live to see it (see "whether we are awake or asleep" [1 Thess. 5:10]).

Then Paul closes this division of the letter by a second thanksgiving (2 Thess. 2:13-17; see 1 Thess. 2:13-16) which not only expresses appropriate gratitude to God, but also serves to reassure the Thessalonian Christians. They need not be "unsettled or alarmed" (2 Thess. 2:2), because God's saving purpose is at work in their lives. They will certainly share in Christ's glory, as they stand fast in the truth and are strengthened by His grace.

11

THE NEED
FOR EXPLANATION

2 Thessalonians 2:1-2

In the pattern already noticed several times in 1 Thessalonians, Paul introduces a new section by addressing his readers as **brothers** [and sisters]. He also immediately indicates his topic: **the coming of our Lord Jesus Christ and our being gathered to him** (2 Thess. 2:1). In this case, the announced topic has two aspects which are closely connected because they are governed by the same single preposition (**concerning**). The two aspects are (1) the **coming of . . . Christ;** and (2) **our being gathered to him.** This close connection between the two is theologically significant because some Bible teachers have proposed prophetic schemes which separate the so-called "Rapture" (**our being gathered to him**) from His later coming in judgment (**destroy by the splendor of his coming** [2:8]). They insert a seven-year period between the two. But Paul, on the other hand, seems here to treat both the **coming of [the] Lord Jesus Christ** and **our being gathered to him** as aspects of a single complex event.

"Being gathered to him" echoes an Old Testament theme—Israel's hope that their scattered exiles would be regathered to their own land (see Deuteronomy 30:4; Isaiah 43:5-6; 49:12). This expectation appears in the teaching of Jesus (see Mark 13:26-27; Matthew 24:31; Luke 13:34). And Paul has recently assured the Thessalonians that their dead in Christ will be included when Christ's people are caught up to meet Him in the air (1 Thess. 4:16-17). Thus, in the words of Ronald Ward, "At the climax of history the Lord will not be without his church, and his church will not be without him."[1]

It appears that some of the Thessalonian converts have formed the notion that the final events of history, summarized under the term **the day**

133

of the Lord (2 Thess. 2:2), are already under way. Of course, they are not thinking of a twenty-four-hour day, but apparently they believe that the last act of human history, the climax of which would be the visible return of Christ, is already in motion. They may be thinking that the last stage is to begin with a period of tribulation, and perhaps interpret their own persecution as a sign that it has begun. As a result they are **unsettled** (2:2); the Greek word used here is a strong word, sometimes used for a ship on a troubled sea. And the verb form of **alarmed** indicates that the excitement and worry were ongoing (2:2).

Paul mentions three possible sources of the misinformation which has caused the mental and spiritual agitation (2:2): it might have been (1) a **prophecy** (the Greek word here means literally "a spirit," but most biblical interpreters take it to mean a supposed word of prophecy, presumably uttered by someone in the congregation; see 1 Corinthians 12:10; 14:29-31; 1 Thessalonians 5:20-21); (2) a **report** (literally "a word," presumably a quoted *oral* statement, because it was distinguished from the next possible source); or (3) a **letter supposed to have come from us** (that is, a written communication wrongly attributed to Paul). Some scholars mention a fourth possibility: a letter which did, in fact, come from Paul, but was misinterpreted. And they have speculated as to how some passage or other from 1 Thessalonians could have been so misunderstood. But clearly, if Paul himself is uncertain how this false notion arose, we are even less likely to solve the puzzle. And obviously, more important than *how* the false notion arose among the Thessalonians, is the correction of their mistaken belief. To that task Paul immediately proceeds.

ENDNOTE

[1]Ronald Ward, *Commentary on 1 and 2 Thessalonians* (Waco, Texas: Word Books, Publisher, 1973), p. 153.

12

THE MAN OF LAWLESSNESS

2 Thessalonians 2:3-12

The bulwark of Paul's argument against the notion that "the day of the Lord has already come" (2 Thess. 2:2) is the fact that the **day** cannot come until a necessary pre-condition has been met—the appearance of the **man of lawlessness,** and **the rebellion** he will instigate (2:3). This Paul develops at some length in a passage which is notorious for the difficulty of its interpretation.

1. HIS COMING AND CHARACTER 2:3-4

Paul begins his argument simply enough: **Don't let anyone deceive you in any way** (2:3). And then, **for** introduces a fact the Thessalonians should remember in order to avoid deception: **that day will not come until. . . .** We may note in passing that the half-brackets in the text of the New International Version indicate that these words have been supplied by the translators. Apparently, in his haste and concern, Paul omitted explicit identification of what must wait **until**. But the context makes it clear that he refers to **the day of the Lord** which, Paul says, cannot take place **until the rebellion occurs.**

The definite article **the** indicates that he is referring to a specific rebellion, an event known to his readers. They know about it because he had informed them when he was among them (2:5). But this creates a problem for modern readers, who have not had that introduction to the topic; here Paul selects from the whole of his teaching on that topic only those aspects necessary for his present purpose of relieving their unfounded anxiety.

The word translated **rebellion** belongs to a word group which begins with the idea of separation or departure and, in the Greek Old Testament and the New Testament, often has a religious connotation (see Joshua 22:22; Jeremiah 2:19; 1 Timothy 4:1; Hebrews 3:12). But the usage here seems to involve more than defection within the realm of religion; it includes the moral and even political.

I. Howard Marshall explains the background against which we should understand the point Paul is making. "In the New Testament there is a general belief that in the last days the opposition of men to God and immorality and wickedness will greatly increase (Matt[hew] 24:12; 2 Tim. 3:1-9). This is associated with an increase in warfare between nations (Mark 13:7f.) and with the activity of false prophets and teachers (Mk. 13:22; 1 Tim. 4:1-3; 2 Tim. 4:3f.) who attempt to lead the church astray; along with all this there is intensified persecution of the church (Mk. 13:9-13). Since Paul can refer to the rebellion as something well known to his readers and requiring no explanation, it is probable that he is here taking up this general motif. . . . reminding his readers that this is an integral part of their expectation for the future."[1]

Paul indicates at least five features which will characterize the **rebellion** he has taught them to expect (2 Thess. 2:3-4).

First, one element is the revelation of **the man of lawlessness.** The term **revealed** implies that he already existed before the public manifestation mentioned here. Presumably **the rebellion** is his doing. His identity is mysterious. He is not Satan, since he will be distinguished from Satan in 1:9, where he is seen as Satan's agent. **Lawlessness** is probably to be understood in terms of 1 John 3:4, "sin is lawlessness," and thus the reading "man of sin," found in some ancient manuscripts (and older English Bible versions, such as the King James Version).

Second, **man doomed to destruction** refers to the lawless one's ultimate fate, as further described in 2 Thessalonians 2:8. Curiously, exactly this same phrase is used of Judas in John 17:12. The implication here is spelled out by F. F. Bruce: "This person is characterized by his opposition to the divine law and therefore is doomed to destruction."[2]

Third, **oppose** and **exalt** (2 Thess. 2:4), literally, "the opposer and self-exalter," probably borrow language from Daniel 7:25 and 11:36, to describe the lawless one's inordinate ambition. Paul emphasizes the extent of the man's self-promotion: over **everything** and everyone— including every so-called deity, every object of worship—he claims total, universal supremacy.

Fourth, **so that** (2 Thess. 2:4, older editions of the New International Version have "and even") indicates the climax of the lawless one's arrogance; **he sets himself up in God's temple.** Interpretation is difficult. Some have thought it a reference to the literal temple then standing in Jerusalem; or, according to some prophetic scenarios, a *rebuilt* temple. Others, noting that the church may be referred to as "the temple of God" (see 2 Corinthians 6:16; also 1 Corinthians 3:16-17; Ephesians 2:21), have taken it to be a reference to an apostate church leader. But it is simpler and probably best to take **sets himself up in God's temple** as a way, which Christians and Jews of that era would readily understand, to express the notion of someone's blasphemously claiming for himself the position, power, and prestige which belong to God alone. This interpretation leads right into the next, and climactic, expression of his arrogance.

Fifth, **proclaiming himself to be God** (2 Thess. 2:4) shows what sitting in the temple implies. There is both biblical and historical background for understanding the significance of this expression. Relevant Old Testament passages include descriptions of the king of Tyre (see Ezekiel 28:1-10) and the king of Babylon (see Isaiah 14:4).

Several episodes in relatively recent Jewish history could be regarded as foreshadowing this predicted event. About 170 B.C., the Seleucid king, Antiochus Epiphanes, arrogantly entered the inner sanctuary of the Temple. The Roman general Pompey did the same in 63 B.C. More recently, in A.D. 41 (thus about ten years before this letter was written), Roman Emperor Gaius ("Caligula") ordered the erection of a statue of himself in the Temple courtyard. Realizing that Jews would engage in suicidal battle against the Roman troops before acceding to such a proposal, King Herod Agrippa (see Acts 12) managed to dissuade the emperor, but not before word of the proposal had sent shock waves through the Jewish population. Facts like these have led I. Howard Marshall to write, "Taking up a motif from Ezekiel and Daniel and given concrete illustrations in previous desecrations of the Jewish temple, both actual and attempted, [Paul] has used this language to portray the character of the culminating manifestation of evil as an anti-theistic power which usurps the place of God in the world."[3]

Obviously, much in this passage lies shrouded in mystery, and probably will remain so until the events themselves make everything clear. Before moving on, mention may be made of another interpretive puzzle. The question arises from comparing the picture of the Second Coming here with that in 1 Thessalonians. It may be asked, "If such a conspicuous figure must arise on the world scene before Christ returns, how can the Second Coming be described as sudden and unexpected?" (see 1 Thessalonians 5:2-3).

Several "resolutions" have been proposed. Some Bible teachers, particularly "dispensationalists," have sought to distinguish two aspects of Christ's return: one *for* believers—the "Rapture" (1 Thess. 4); and a second one after the "Tribulation," *with* believers (2 Thess. 2).[4] Also, many scholars have pointed out that descriptions of the end times in Scripture do not readily yield to the logical organization modern Western minds crave. For example, Leon Morris states that "it is a commonplace in apocalyptic [end times] literature that the Lord's coming is to be sudden, and yet that it will be preceded by signs. We find this in the Gospels and Revelation, to name no other."[5] Another approach alleviates the pro·lem by maintaining that it is only unbelievers who will be surprised (1 ? ιess. 5); believers will discern the signs of the times (2 Thess. 2:3), thougl their sin-blinded contemporaries will not (2:9-12).

2. HIS PRESENT RESTRAINING 2:5-7

Don't you remember . . . (2 Thess. 2:5). Paul breaks off to remind them that these things should not be new to them. He had instructed them on these matters when he was among them, apparently more than once, as indicated by **used to tell** (see 1 Thessalonians 5:1). Evidently these were regular topics in his standard teaching to new believers (1 Thess. 1:9-10; 4:1-2; 5:1). Therefore, Paul is recalling only the highlights necessary to refute the false notions circulating among them, and, as mentioned above, this is a major factor of our difficulty in understanding him now.

Incidentally, we may observe that this is the only use of "I" in this letter, except for a final note (3:17). This raises an interesting question. Should we infer that Paul, rather than his associates, was their primary teacher? Perhaps the teaching was thought of as his, even if transmitted through his colleagues on the missionary team.

The next two verses (2:6-7), present another nest of interpretive problems; they are among the most difficult in the New Testament. The problems begin with the first two words: **and now** (2:6). The question is whether **now** is merely *transitional,* indicating the shift to a new topic, or *temporal,* signifying, "You know what is holding him NOW," that is, at the present time, and not later. The **till** in the next verse seems to favor the second option, as does **at the proper time** (2:6) and also "then" (2:8).

The really difficult question is, **what** (2:6) or "who" (2:7) is holding back the man of lawlessness? Traditionally, evangelical scholars have supported one or another of three proposed "solutions."

One answer is the Holy Spirit. Some students of the Bible have seen the variation just noticed between neuter (**what**) of 2:6 and masculine (**who**) of 2:7, as the clue which points to the Holy Spirit as the restrainer, the one holding back the lawless one and his works. For in the Greek language, the word for "spirit" is grammatically neuter, but when a pronoun is used for the Third Person of the Trinity, it is the masculine, "he" (for example, John 15:26). And, further, the restraint of evil might logically be expected to be one of His functions, though there is little direct biblical evidence, except on the personal level (see Acts 7:51; Galatians 5:17-18). There are at least two significant difficulties with this view. First, it is difficult to understand why Paul should be reticent about identifying the Holy Spirit as the restrainer. Second, the main problem is understanding how and why He will be **taken out of the way** (2 Thess. 2:7). The most frequently used hypothesis is that, in some significant (but unspecified) sense, He "leaves" the world when the church is "raptured out."

A second view, widely held, is that the restraining power is the Roman government—the emperor (masculine) or the empire (neuter). In support of this view an appeal is made to Romans. 13:1-7. Some have thought this view of imperial authority was confirmed in Paul's own experience because, on several occasions, Roman authorities protected Paul from the enemies of the gospel. However, no instances of that sort are recorded in Acts as occurring *before* the writing of this letter (with one possible exception—Gallio's favorable ruling [Acts 18:12-17], which *might* have occurred by that time. Of course, the Thessalonian letters *were* written from Corinth). One strength of this view is that the reason for Paul's reticence about identification of the restrainer becomes obvious. It would not have been wise to speak openly of the emperor's removal. But the major, and perhaps fatal, consideration is the fact that the Roman emperor and empire have long since "been taken out of the way," and still the man of lawlessness has not appeared.

A third possibility is that the restraining power is not the Roman Empire as such, but rather the *principle* of law and order which was then exemplified by the Roman Empire, and later by other civil authorities. This interpretation may fit with indications elsewhere in Scripture of a general abandonment of civil control at the time of the second coming of Christ.

Several other, less-than-convincing suggestions have been made. Leon Morris provides the bottom line: "The plain fact is that Paul and his readers knew what he was talking about, and we do not. . . . It is best that we frankly acknowledge our ignorance. The important thing is that some power was in operation and that the Man of Lawlessness could not possibly put in his appearance until this power was removed."[6] In any case, the important fact remains and is all we need: the whole of our ongoing history is under God's control, as **at the proper time** affirms. He is in charge of the whole process (John 19:11; Acts 4:28).

The **For** which begins 2 Thessalonians 2:7 suggests that Paul intends further explanation, but there are so many unknown elements that, for modern readers, it is not very illuminating. Perhaps he means that the person/principle of rebellion against God is already operating against the gospel (for example, in the persecution of the Thessalonians), but is not yet openly enthroned as he will be for a brief time at the end. Paul's contemporary, the Apostle John declared in his first epistle, "the spirit of the antichrist" (1 John 4:3) was already at work (1 John 2:18).

John Stott believes that he/it is certainly active in our day: "We detect its subversive influence around us today—in the atheistic stance of secular humanism, in totalitarian tendencies of extreme left-wing and right-wing ideologies, in the materialism of the consumer society which puts things in the place of God, in those so-called 'theologies' which proclaim the death of God, and the end of moral absolutes, and in the social permissiveness which cheapens the sanctity of human life, sex, marriage and family, all of which God created or instituted."[7]

3. HIS REVELATION AND DESTRUCTION 2:8-12

After the parenthetical explanations of 2 Thessalonians 2:5-7, Paul returns with verse 8 to the time period of verses 3 and 4, and brings us to the next stage in the end-time drama—the revelation of **the lawless one** (2:8). Paul notes the rebel's arrival on the scene (2:8a), but quickly turns attention to Christ and His victory (2:8b), and then closes this segment by describing further the final activities of the rebel and the destiny of his followers (2:9-12).

No details are given concerning the revelation of the man of lawlessness. Apparently they are not necessary for the present purpose. Paul simply states that the rebel's revelation will be followed by his destruction. It should be noted that the **revealed** used of him three times in this context (2:3, 6, 8) is the same Greek term used, in noun form, of the Lord Jesus in 1:7. This may suggest that the lawless one is a usurper, intending to claim the mantle which belongs to the true Messiah (another clue that he may be the person elsewhere called "Antichrist"). But the divine Sovereign prevails. Evil, personified, comes to climactic expression according to God's plan and schedule, only to be dealt with decisively.

The Lord Jesus will overthrow and **destroy** the rebel, first **with the breath of his mouth.** Some interpreters think that this last expression shows the ease of His victory—there is no struggle. The Lord destroys, as He created, with **the breath of his mouth** (see Genesis 2:7). Others see the image of war and/or divine judgment; His breath is a weapon (see Revelation 19:15). Probably there is an allusion to Isaiah 11:4 (see Exodus 15:8; Job 4:9).

Also, **The Lord Jesus** conquers **by the splendor of his coming.** The two nouns here, **splendor** and **coming,** are almost synonyms, and both are special terms often used for the visible manifestation of a divine figure. William Arndt and Wilbur Gingrich say of the Greek word translated "splendor" here, "As a religious technical term it means a visible manifestation of a hidden divinity."[8] This is the word from which English derives *epiphany,* and it characterizes the return of Christ as a "public manifestation" (see 1 Timothy 6:14; 2 Timothy 4:1, 8; Titus 2:13; in 2 Timothy 1:10 it refers to the Incarnation[9]). **Coming** is *parousia* (see comments on 1 Thessalonians 2:19; 4:13–5:11). It is not clear why the two almost synonymous terms are doubled up here; perhaps for emphasis on the completeness of Christ's victory. No details of the conflict are given. Perhaps it is all over very quickly.

Interestingly, *parousia* is also used for the **coming of the lawless one** (2 Thess. 2:9a). The use of the same word may be intended to indicate that his coming is a sort of imitation of the coming of Christ; he is a Satanic counterfeit. Neither here nor anywhere else does Paul use the word "Antichrist" explicitly, but the idea seems to be present.

Verse 8 had indicated the doom of **the lawless one,** but now verses 9 and 10 move back in time to describe his brief, meteoric career in terms of (1) his inspiration; (2) his methods; and (3) the result.

First, Satan will make **the lawless one** his dedicated instrument in a manner parallel to the way Jesus was totally devoted to doing His Father's will (John 5:17, 30; 17:4). This means that, as God was powerfully at work in and through Jesus, so Satan will be powerfully at work in "the lawless one" (Rev. 13:2b, 4).

Second, the man's methods will involve **counterfeit miracles, signs and wonders** (2 Thess. 2:9). The same three terms (without the "counterfeit," of course) are used, singly and combined, at various points in the Gospels to describe the works of Jesus.[10] The three appear together in Acts 2:22, where they are said to have shown Jesus to be "accredited by God." Some of the same terms are used in Paul's statement concerning God's vindication of his own apostleship (see Romans 15:18-19; 2 Corinthians 12:12; also Acts 15:12).

Third, the results are the opposite, of course. Whereas Christ's miracles were in the interests of righteousness and truth, the rebel's activities serve evil and result in deception. Righteousness uses truth to lead to salvation; unrighteousness uses deceit to lead to destruction (see Mark 13:22; Revelation 13:13).

The phrase **counterfeit miracles** ("pretended signs" [Revised Standard Version]; "lying wonders" [New Revised Standard Version]) is somewhat difficult. The literal translation of the Greek would be "wonders of a lie," and the meaning is not absolutely clear. The phrase *could* mean that the supposed miracles are trickery; it *may* point to the deceiver, Satan, as their origin; it *probably* indicates their purpose. All of these interpretations could be true, of course, for they are not mutually contradictory. In any case, the description is what might be expected for one who is an agent of Satan, "the father of lies" (John 8:44). Whatever their exact nature, the purpose of these miracles is to establish the religious claims of the rebel and/or his agents who perform them, a deceitful imitation of the credentials of true apostles.

Second Thessalonians 2:10 continues the description of the work of Satan through the lawless one and his agents. He is the arch deceiver, and he succeeds among **those who are perishing.** The last phrase reminds of other passages which divide humanity into two categories of persons moving in opposite directions (for example, 1 Cor. 1:18; 2 Cor. 2:15; 4:3; see 1 Corinthians 2:14). In the past, extreme Calvinists have sought to use passages like this in support of a doctrine of "double predestination" (the belief that from all eternity God chose some for heaven, and determined to pass by others; for example, Louis Berkhof says "predestination includes two parts, namely, election and reprobation, the predetermination of both the good and the wicked to their final end. . . .").[11]

But here Paul does not attribute the destiny of the lost to the inscrutable will of God; verse 10b makes it clear the persons here described have chosen the path of destruction for themselves. The rest of the paragraph, describing the fate of the followers of the lawless one and the reason for that destiny, maintains the characteristic biblical tension, affirming both divine sovereignty and human freedom.

They perish because they refused to love the truth or, more literally, "they did not welcome the love of the truth." In other words, they loved darkness rather than light (John 3:19-21). **And so be saved** (literally, "unto being saved") indicates the divine purpose in sending Jesus, the light of the world. But human freedom can frustrate that purpose. As F. F. Bruce puts it, "To receive the love of the truth is the way of salvation; to refuse it means perdition."[12]

For this reason God sends them a powerful delusion (2 Thess. 2:11). God makes His truth known, and when people deliberately and persistently reject it, the time comes that "God gives them up" (Rom. 1:18-32) and the result is blindness as a form of divine judgment. For those who close their eyes to truth, the ultimate result is spiritual blindness. The principle operates even in the natural world: an unused organ atrophies. When a cast is removed from what had been a broken leg, the muscles are initially weak and flabby. The Hindu devotee who keeps his arm in a fixed position for a long period of time eventually loses his use of it.

Light is given to be used, and when it is, the one who has, will receive even more (Mark 4:21-25). But the opposite principle also applies, and this is God's doing: **God sends.** Ernest Best says, "God intervenes with definite action; in Rom. 1:24, 26, 28 the rejection of God is punished with sin, that is, each stage in sin leads on to a further stage, and this takes place by God's action (see Ps[alm] 81:11f.). . . ."[13]

The rather bold statement of the divine purpose is startling: **so that they will believe the lie and so that all will be condemned** (2 Thess. 2:11b-12a). The Greek is, literally, "unto believing the lie"; grammatically it is parallel to "unto being saved" at the end of verse 10. Having rejected the truth, they have opened themselves up to falsehood, have become gullible and are now deceived by the signs and wonders of the rebel (Rom. 1:25). Does this help to account for the fact that even educated and intelligent people subscribe to New Age ideas, and even believe that somehow their lives are affected by their astrological sign?

Second Thessalonians 2:12 indicates the divine justice which underlies this aspect of God's governance of the universe. The cause of the condemnation spoken of here is stated negatively, **have not believed the truth,** and positively, **have delighted in wickedness.** The last phrase indicates that the people involved are not the victims of ignorance nor of adverse circumstances. They have gladly chosen wickedness. And the Greek word **delighted,** says A. L. Moore, "signifies a positive approval (see NEB [New English Bible] 'their deliberate choice') and a sense of contentment with the approved object or person."[14] Obviously, there are difficult theological truths in the background here as we seek properly to relate the biblical doctrines of election and of human responsibility. But there is nothing here to contradict the overall scriptural truth: If in the end we are saved, it is God's doing; if in the end we are lost, we ourselves are responsible.

And concerning the larger picture in this section (2:3-12), with its selected elements from the final scene of human history, Leon Morris offers a helpful perspective: "[Paul's] purpose is to meet the need of his friends, not to satisfy their (or our) curiosity. His unfolding of the picture is not with a view to providing them with a timetable of events at the end so that they will be in a position to anticipate the course of events step by step. He writes to assure them that whatever happens, God is over all: God is working out his purposes and will continue to do so until the very end. The Man of Lawlessness and the great rebellion must be mentioned, but Paul's interest is not in them. His interest is in God and the working out of God's purpose."[15]

ENDNOTES

[1]I. Howard Marshall, *1 and 2 Thessalonians,* New Century Bible Commentary (Grand Rapids, Michigan: Wm. B. Eerdmans Publishing Co., 1983), p. 189

[2]F. F. Bruce, *1 and 2 Thessalonians,* Word Biblical Commentary (Waco, Texas: Word Books, Publisher, 1982), p. 167.

[3]Marshall, pp. 191–92.

[4]Dispensationalism is a scheme of biblical interpretation which arose in mid-nineteenth-century England and spread to America in the late nineteenth and early twentieth centuries. It was popularized by its pervasive presence in the notes of the once-popular Scofield Bible. In the absence of detailed prophetic schemes in the evangelical Arminian tradition, some Wesleyans have borrowed bits and pieces of a dispensationalist interpretation of end times, but it is fair to say that the majority of The Wesleyan Church's biblical scholars and theologians regard dispensationalism as incompatible with Wesleyanism.

[5]Leon Morris, *The First and Second Epistles to the Thessalonians,* rev. ed., New International Commentary on the New Testament (Grand Rapids, Michigan: Wm. B. Eerdmans Publishing Co., 1991), p. 20.

[6]Morris, p. 228.

[7]John Stott, *The Gospel and the End of Time* (Downers Grove, Illinois: InterVarsity Press, 1991), p. 171.

[8]William F. Arndt and F. Wilbur Gingrich, *A Greek-English Lexicon of the New Testament* (Chicago, Illinois: The University of Chicago Press, 1957), p. 304.

[9]The Incarnation was God's coming to us in the person of Jesus.

[10]The Gospels include the New Testament books of Matthew, Mark, Luke, and John.

[11]Louis Berkhof, *Systematic Theology* (Grand Rapids, Michigan: Wm. B. Eerdmans Publishing Co., 1941), p. 113.

[12]Bruce, p. 174.

[13]Ernest Best, *A Commentary on the First and Second Epistles to the Thessalonians,* Harper's New Testament Commentaries (New York: Harper and Row Publishers, 1972), p. 309.

[14]A. L. Moore, *1 and 2 Thessalonians,* Century Bible (London: Thomas Nelson and Sons, Ltd., 1969), p. 106.

[15]Morris, p. 230.

13

ASSURANCE OF SALVATION

2 Thessalonians 2:13-17

N ow, no doubt gladly, Paul turns from contemplating the destiny of followers of the man of lawlessness, to his certainty concerning the salvation of his Thessalonian converts. He wants to communicate his confidence before God concerning their salvation, present and future, in such a way that they will experience the **good hope** (2 Thess. 2:16) which is part of their Christian birthright.

These relatively new Christians find themselves in the midst of persecution from outside the group, and within the camp there has been instability and alarm caused by mistaken notions concerning the Day of the Lord. He has provided perspective on both those issues (persecution in 1:5-10 and inappropriate alarm in 2:3-11), and now he wants to focus their attention on the saving purpose of God which was already at work in their lives, and to do so in a way which would build up their confidence. He does it by expressing his thanksgiving to God concerning them (2:13-14), by exhorting them to perseverance (2:15), and by letting them "hear" his prayer in their behalf (2:16-17).

1. PAUL GIVES THANKS FOR THEM 2:13-14

Here, as in 1 Thessalonians 2:13-16, we have a second expression in this letter of thanksgiving for the Thessalonian converts, and, as in 2 Thessalonians 1:3, Paul acknowledges it to be a duty (**ought**), although again without any sense of burdensomeness. In the Greek, **we** receives emphasis, and this *may* put a subtle twist in the thought; if they, the Thessalonians, are too discouraged at the moment to feel the proper level of gratitude to God, at least their missionaries feel the need to express *their* thanks to Him.

147

And the focus of their gratitude at the moment is precisely for the Thessalonian Christians, specifically for what they have become, in Christ—**brothers loved by the Lord** (2:13). This echoes almost the same expression in 1 Thessalonians 1:4, and in both cases their membership in the family of God is traced to their being chosen by God. Here it is taken a step further back—to their being **loved by the Lord.** As mentioned before, **Lord,** without further definition, usually refers to Christ in Paul's letters. That is clearly so here, because Paul explicitly names **God** as subject of the next verb. (If **Lord** meant "God," Paul simply would have said, *"He* **chose.")**

The specific motive for thanksgiving here is God's electing grace: **because from the beginning God chose you to be saved.** Given the situation of the Thessalonian believers, this is an especially helpful reminder because, as Ernest Best declares, "The belief of Christians in their election has often been an important element enabling them to endure trial and persecution steadfastly, as Paul obviously intends it to be here."[1] **Beginning** here probably refers to God's purpose from eternity (see Ephesians 1:4; 2 Timothy 1:9; also 1 Corinthians 2:7) because some further explanation would have been required if Paul had meant, for example, from the beginning of his ministry among them. That their salvation was an aspect of God's eternal purpose was intended to be reassuring to these new Christians.

As the New International Version footnote indicates, rather than **from the beginning,** some ancient documents read "as his firstfruits." Paul does use the latter expression occasionally, but almost always with an additional phrase which provides further definition (for example, Romans 16:5—literally, "firstfruit of Asia for Christ." The evidence for choosing between the two readings is rather evenly balanced, and scholars remain divided. The thrust of the paragraph as a whole is not significantly affected by the choice of one or the other.

In any case, Paul affirms here that the goal of God's choice is that they should be **saved.** Paul probably intends a deliberate contrast to the **perishing** of 2 Thessalonians 2:10, and, as well, he wishes to reassure them in the midst of their ongoing persecution. In a context like this, salvation denotes a *process* which has a divine side—**the sanctifying work of the Spirit**—but also involves human responsibility—**through belief in the truth.** This last, too, contrasts with the persons who **have not believed the truth** (2:10b-12).

Paul's assurance concerning God's purpose for them is further strengthened by his reminding them that God **called** (2:14) them. This underlines again God's initiative in salvation, but also shows that He followed through. He **chose** (2:13) and then He implemented that choice: he **called.** The dynamic effect of the divine call was clearly indicated in the first letter, especially in 5:24, where the intention to encourage is especially plain (see 1 Thessalonians 2:12; and comments on 2:12 and 5:24).

God communicated His call to the Thessalonians **through our gospel** (2 Thess. 2:14). It was He who sent the evangelistic team to Thessalonica (see Acts 16:6-10). It is worth stating plainly an implication here: recognition of the doctrine of election does not eliminate the need for evangelism. God's heavenly purposes are often wrought out on earth, in human history, through His obedient servants; for that matter, sometimes even by disobedient servants (for example, Jonah), not to mention unbelievers (for example, Cyrus; see Isaiah 44:28).

The divine purpose, as described here, is **that you might share in the glory of our Lord Jesus Christ.** This is a reminder that our "salvation" has dimensions which we, in this present life, cannot adequately imagine. The glory of God, forfeited by humankind in the fall (see Romans 3:23), by the grace of God (Rom. 3:24-26) has been brought back within the reach of faith (2 Cor. 4:4, 6), by the life, death, and resurrection of Christ. It may be experienced now, step-by-step (2 Cor. 3:18), but will be fully realized only at the End (1 Cor. 15:43; 2 Thess. 1:12; see also Philippians 3:21; 1 Thessalonians 2:12). (Note the stages marked out in Romans 8:30: "predestined, called, justified, glorified.")

Of course, this sharing in His glory is not something to which we are automatically entitled, nor is it something we earn. The Greek word translated "share" here is rendered "receive" in 1 Thessalonians 5:9-10, where our salvation is "through the Lord Jesus Christ," and is the consequence of His death "for us." We do not "earn," but human response *is* required and, therefore, Paul turns to exhortation.

2. PAUL EXHORTS THEM 2:15

Now, from the thanksgiving, which was phrased in such a way as also to serve as a powerful encouragement, Paul turns to admonition. We must note how balanced is Paul's theology; in healthy tension with the emphasis on the eternal divine purpose is this exhortation calling for the Thessalonians' active response. The contents of 2 Thessalonians 2:13-14 serve to reassure, but also to stir them to action.

So then (2:15) signals the logical conclusion, the practical application of the gospel truth Paul has just summarized (2:13-14). Affectionately addressing them again as **brothers,** he urges them to **stand firm** and to **hold to the teachings.** Both verbs are in the form which signifies continuation: keep on standing and holding. The need for the first may reflect their situation ("persecutions and trials" [1:4]; "unsettled or alarmed" [2:2]), and the second may be the means to the first; that is, stand firm *by* holding on.

The object of their firm grip is **the teachings we passed on to you.** As the New International Version footnote shows, the word translated **teachings** can also be rendered *traditions,* and, in a context like this, the word refers to the basic elements of instruction which the missionary church planters regularly passed along to their converts as the God-given basis for their new Christian lives. Some of the "traditions" would be doctrinal in nature (for example, 1 Thessalonians 2:13; 4:1-2; 1 Corinthians 15:3-8); some would pertain to Christian life (for example, Colossians 2:6-7; 1 Corinthians 4:17; 11:2, 23-34).

This term, then, emphasizes continuity in the passing along of Christian truth (clearer when translated *tradition*); this is truth which was contained in the apostolic message, and behind it is the authority of Jesus Christ. John Stott defines what the command here means for us today: "To 'stand firm and hold to the teachings' means in our case to be biblical and evangelical Christians, to be uncompromisingly loyal to the teaching of Christ and his apostles."[2]

Such authoritative teaching the Thessalonians had received from Paul and his evangelistic team, both **by word of mouth** and **by letter**—orally when they were with them, but also in writing (for example, 1 Thessalonians, and now this present letter). Their security for the future lay with abiding in these truths.

But this is not a project just for the individual Christian. Noting that **brothers** recurs so soon (2 Thess. 2:13, 15), John Stott warns against "lone ranger" Christianity and declares, "In other words, we need each other. The church is the fellowship of faith, the society for sacred study, the [interpretative] community. In it we receive teaching from pastors who are duly authorized to expound the tradition of the apostles, we wrestle together with contemporary application, and we teach and admonish each other out of the same Scriptures. . . . So we need the checks and balances of the Christian family, in order to help restrain our rampant individualism and establish us in the truth."[3]

3. PAUL PRAYS FOR THEM 2:16-17

And now Paul closes this section by turning to prayer. He has been reminding them of their duty, but, of course, they cannot carry it through without God's enabling. But they may pray confidently, assured that God who has called them to participate in the glory of Christ is prepared to see them through.

The sequence of names in the prayer's address, **our Lord Jesus Christ himself and God our Father** (2 Thess. 2:16), is unusual but not unique (for example, Galatians 1:1; 2 Corinthians 13:14). The reason for the order is not obvious; perhaps it reflects the christological emphasis in 2 Thessalonians 2:13 through 3:5, where the Lord Jesus is mentioned more often than the Father. The Greek behind **loved** and **gave** indicates reference to definite past actions, most likely to Christ's atoning death (see Romans 5:8), as an expression of the divine love which characterizes both Father and Son. Notice that Paul has switched, just for one verse (2 Thess. 2:16), from second to first person—that is, from **you** to **us**—as if he cannot bear to mention the divine love without testifying that he, too, has experienced the love of God in Christ (Gal. 2:20).

The actual petition (after a long introduction) is that Christ and His Father might **encourage . . . and strengthen** (2 Thess. 2:17) the Thessalonian converts, requests that are directly relevant to their situation: their confusion and concern about Last Things, their experience of continuing persecution, the general moral atmosphere in which they were called to live out their Christian witness.

The basis of their encouragement is the divine **grace,** which is rooted in the divine **love** from the God who is **our Father** and Jesus Christ who is **our Lord** and, therefore, the **encouragement** here partakes of the **eternal.** F. F. Bruce observes that "the grace is God's, the hope is ours, given us by his grace. It is because he gives his people 'good (such as well-founded) hope' that he is 'the God of hope' (Rom. 15:13)."[4]

But, we must notice that this encouragement was intended to strengthen for **every good deed and word.** The reality of their inward faith was to be exhibited in their visible conduct (see 2 Corinthians 9:8; Ephesians 2:10; Colossians 1: 10; 3:17; 1 Timothy 2:10; 2 Timothy 2:21; 3:17; Titus 3:1). As we have said before, reflection on the Second Coming in the New Testament leads, not to speculation, but appropriate action. I. Howard Marshall writes, "The whole section on the future and its problems closes with a prayer for a Christian hope based on the experience of the love of God and issuing in a fruitful life; apocalyptic [end-time] speculation has disappeared from view."[5]

ENDNOTES

[1]Ernest Best, *A Commentary on the First and Second Epistles to the Thessalonians,* Harper's New Testament Commentaries (New York: Harper and Row Publishers, 1972), p. 312.

[2]John Stott, *The Gospel and the End of Time* (Downers Grove, Illinois: InterVarsity Press, 1991), p. 178.

[3]Ibid., pp. 178–9.

[4]F. F. Bruce, *1 and 2 Thessalonians,* Word Biblical Commentary (Waco, Texas: Word Books, Publisher, 1982), p. 196.

[5]I. Howard Marshall, *1 and 2 Thessalonians,* New Century Bible Commentary (Grand Rapids, Michigan: Wm. B. Eerdmans Publishing Co., 1983), p. 212.

Part Five

EXHORTATION

2 Thessalonians 3:1-18

In the remainder of 2 Thessalonians, the structure is somewhat puzzling. This third main division starts off with the missionaries requesting prayer for themselves and their ministry (3:1-5), a topic which, in other Pauline writings, comes at the close of the letter. In the preceding section Paul had provided some words of encouragement for the Thessalonian believers and then prayed for them (2:13-17). Now, after a request for prayer for themselves (3:1-2), he again offers assurances and once more prays on their behalf (3:3-5).

Then, abruptly, at 3:6, Paul launches into a very different topic, calling upon the congregation to discipline idlers in their midst (3:6-15). There has been no preparation for such a directive in this letter, although the subject was touched upon in the first letter. It is obvious that Paul feels strongly about this issue (twice, in quick succession, he invokes "the Lord Jesus Christ"); one might wonder why he has waited until now to broach the subject. Possibly he had only recently received a report (**We hear** [3:11]).

14

MUTUAL CONCERN EXPRESSED

2 Thessalonians 3:1-5

On occasion, Paul uses **finally** to introduce the last main topic of a letter, even when he is not really near the end of the letter. Sometimes he includes several other matters (see 1 Thessalonians 4:1; Philippians 3:1; 4:8). Here, the word introduces a kind of exchange of prayer concerns between the missionary team and a congregation they have founded.

1. REQUEST FOR PRAYER 3:1-2

Evidently, Paul believes that their Thessalonian converts are already engaged in intercession on their behalf; the form of the verb **pray** (2 Thess. 3:1) suggests this: **keep on praying** as you are doing, regularly. His request here is not unique; he will often seek such prayer support (for example, Romans 15:30; Ephesians 6:18-19; Colossians 4:3; Philemon 22; see 2 Corinthians 1:11; Philippians 1:19).

The content of the prayer request is twofold. First, he prays that the gospel may spread swiftly and successfully. **The message of the Lord,** or more literally "the word of the Lord," is the good news of which God is the author and His grace is the subject matter; it is the Word which "rang out" from the Thessalonians (1 Thess. 1:8), but now needs to be proclaimed everywhere. Second, Paul asks for prayer that in the service of that message, he and his missionary team may not be hindered in their ministry by evil men. The second request is actually in support of the first.

Spread rapidly is, more literally, "speed on" ("run swiftly and be glorified" [New King James Version]), and probably reflects the language of Psalm 147:15 (see Isaiah 55:11; Psalm 19:5; Romans 10:18).

Also Paul can use "run" to refer to his own apostolic mission (see Galatians 2:2; 1 Corinthians 9:24; see also Philippians 2:16, where the Greek word is different).

And be honored describes the desired response, the recognition in the hearts and minds of the gospel's hearers that this is the Word of the living God, which they now receive with joyous faith. For example, this was precisely the response among the Gentile hearers of the Word in Pisidian Antioch (see Acts 13:48, where the same Greek word occurs). The Word thus honored is effective to transform lives, even as it had been working in the lives of the Thessalonian believers (1 Thess. 2:13). John Wesley understood **honored** to mean "acknowledged as divine, and bring forth much fruit."[1]

Just as it was with you indicates that the Thessalonians' own receptivity to the gospel was a "model" for others (1 Thess. 1:6-7), and served to spread the word in two provinces of the Roman Empire (1 Thess. 1:8-9).

It should be noted that the form of the Greek words translated **spread** and **be honored** signifies an ongoing process, eventually "to the ends of the earth." But the ever-present threat of a hindrance to that process prompts the second part of the prayer request. There are many unbelievers in the world (**not everyone has faith**) and some of them are **wicked and evil** (2 Thess. 3:2). (The two words are nearly synonymous, but **wicked** perhaps adds the thought of being *perverse*.) Such persons oppose the spread of the gospel, and often that opposition takes the form of striking at the gospel's messengers. In fact, it is probable that even as he was writing, Paul was experiencing problems in Corinth (Acts 18:6, 12). And certainly on other occasions in the course of his ministry, he needed to request prayer support in dangerous situations (Rom. 15:31; 2 Cor. 1:10-11).

Earlier in this letter, Paul had warned that a worldwide spiritual battle was in progress; "the secret power of lawlessness is already at work" (2 Thess. 2:7). In that context, this apostolic call for prayer stands as a reminder of the importance of the church's ministry of intercession for all who are engaged in evangelism and missions. In the words of A. L. Moore, "The request for prayer recognizes the participation of all Christians in the church's mission, and that it is not the prerogative or responsibility only of those who preach or teach."[2]

2. ASSURANCE FOR THE THESSALONIANS 3:3-5

But Paul does not dwell on his own problems. Thinking of threats by evil men, his pastoral heart goes quickly to the needs of the Thessalonian converts. Therefore, he shifts rather abruptly from prayer requests for themselves to reassurances for the Thessalonian Christians. There is intermingling of thanksgiving, exhortation, and prayer similar to that of 2 Thessalonians 2:13-17. Separated from the congregation and unable to return for the time being, Paul is concerned for the young congregation, under threat from Satan and his agents (2:9-10), experiencing continuing persecution (1:5) and subject to attack by **the evil one** (3:3).

But the Lord is faithful. The confidence which alleviates Paul's anxiety about his own danger also provides a springboard for launching into reassuring reminders for the Thessalonians. The ground of his confidence is **the Lord,** the God whose he is and whom he serves (see Acts 27:23). Most interpreters agree that here (3:3; and in 3:4-5), as well as elsewhere in the New Testament, **Lord,** without further definition, refers to Christ, whom Paul believes to be utterly trustworthy. He knows that "the Lord is to be trusted" (New English Bible; see 1 Corinthians 1:9; 10:13; 2 Corinthians 1:18; 1 Thessalonians 5:24, where the faithfulness is attributed to *God,* but Paul has already placed God the Father and the Lord Jesus Christ side-by-side; see also 1 Thessalonians 1:1; 2 Thessalonians 1:1; 2:16.)

The Lord will provide what the Thessalonian converts need—in this case, their need for strength and protection. The assurance that God **will strengthen** has already been given (2:17; 1 Thess. 3:2, 13). And Scripture pledges God's protection for His own (Ps. 12:7; 121:7; 141:8-9; and especially John 17:15). From whom or what do they need protection? The label **the evil one** is somewhat ambiguous; the reference could be impersonal—evil in general—or it could mean Satan. Since Satan's activity lies behind all evil, perhaps the difference is not great. But there are several considerations which suggest that the New International Version's rendering, **the evil one,** is what Paul intended. First, the activity of Satan as threatening the well-being of the Thessalonian Christians is noted elsewhere in these letters (2:9; 1 Thess. 2:18; 3:5). Second, the immediate context (2 Thess. 3:1-5), with its interaction on several levels "feels" more personal. Third, it was the practice of early Christians to use this term for Satan (see Matthew 13:19, 38; Ephesians 6:16; 1 John 2:13-14; 5:18-19).

This means that the Thessalonian converts are in a situation of danger (see 1 Peter 5:8), but, in another rapid shift, Paul expresses no anxiety but rather declares his complete **confidence** that the Thessalonians **are doing and will continue to do** everything he asks (2 Thess. 3:4). That confidence is based on two considerations. First, they and he are **in the Lord.** That means, says F. F. Bruce, that "the writers trust the Lord to maintain in those believers the good work he has manifestly begun," and then he enumerates parallel uses in Romans 14:14; Galatians 5:10; Philippians 2:24.[3] And second, the Lord is obviously the ultimate basis of Paul's confidence, but there is another indication: the conduct, to date, of most of the Thessalonian converts. For the most part, they are following Paul's teachings, and, therefore, he has every reason to believe that they **will continue to do the things we command** (2 Thess. 3:4). They have recognized his apostleship and, therefore, his authority over them.

Command is a strong word, military in tone. The form of the verb indicates that he believes that Paul has the right and the duty, even now at a distance, to issue orders and not merely to make recommendations. **Command** occurred in 1 Thessalonians 4:11, where it was translated "told," and in noun form in 4:2 (translated "instructions"). Here it will reappear in verses 6, 10 ("rule") and 12. In using the word, consciously or unconsciously, Paul is moving toward the instructions he is about to give.

But before giving any more orders, Paul will pray for them, pray to the One he has just described as the **Lord** and **faithful,** He who will **strengthen** and **protect.** Such a theology fosters **confidence** in both the one who teaches in His name and those who are being discipled. He prays for their spiritual development in language which may reflect the thought of the Christian life as following in the "way" of salvation. The word translated **direct** occurs also in 1 Thessalonians 3:11 ("clear the way") and means not so much "guide" as "open up the path and move along" these Thessalonians into **God's love and Christ's perseverance** (2 Thess. 3:5). He prays concerning their **hearts,** which, in a context like this, means their whole inner being.

A. L. Moore notes similar language in the Greek Old Testament renderings of 1 Chronicles 29:18; and 2 Chronicles 12:14; 19:3; 20:33, "where it signifies a dedication of the whole personality towards the attainment of some goal. Here the meaning is . . . that he will keep the converts firmly set upon their path toward the attainment of two goals, love of God and the steadfastness of Christ. . . ."[4]

It should be acknowledged that there is some ambiguity in two key phrases: **God's love** could mean (1) God's love for us or (2) our love for Him; and **perseverance of Christ** could mean (1) the perseverance He displayed or (2) our perseverance in relation to Him. The New International

Version's translation, **God's love** and **perseverance of Christ,** indicates their interpretation in favor of the first alternative in both cases. This would be the consensus among New Testament scholars, such as I. Howard Marshall, who says, "The readers are to participate in the love shown by God and the steadfastness shown by Christ. The thought is of steadfastness in the midst of afflictions."[5] It would be fair to add, however, that the alternative renderings are not out of the picture altogether, for surely Paul knows that the experience of God's love will generate an answering love for Him on the part of believers, even as reflection on the perseverance of Christ will stimulate their faithfulness to Him.

ENDNOTES

[1]John Wesley, *Explanatory Notes upon the New Testament* (London: Epworth Press, 1950), p. 768.

[2]A. L. Moore, *1 and 2 Thessalonians,* Century Bible (London: Thomas Nelson and Sons, Ltd., 1969), p. 111.

[3]F. F. Bruce, *1 and 2 Thessalonians,* Word Biblical Commentary (Waco, Texas: Word Books, Publisher, 1982), p. 200.

[4]Moore, p. 114.

[5]I. Howard Marshall, *1 and 2 Thessalonians,* New Century Bible Commentary (Grand Rapids, Michigan: Wm. B. Eerdmans Publishing Co., 1983), p. 218.

INSTRUCTION
CONCERNING THE IDLE
2 Thessalonians 3:6-15

Before closing the letter, the missionary team needs to address one remaining issue. They had given detailed and authoritative oral instructions on Christian lifestyle in the course of their first visit to the Thessalonians (1 Thess. 4:1-2). And they had reiterated in the earlier letter the need for the Thessalonian converts to work to support themselves rather than living in idleness (1 Thess. 4:11-12; 5:14). But now reports that Paul and his colleagues have been receiving (2 Thess. 3:11) have made them know that they need to expand on the earlier teaching and to call for its reinforcement by appropriate disciplinary procedures.

The precise nature of the problem is not entirely clear, and its root cause difficult to determine. Although Paul does not make an explicit connection, it has been widely held that the Thessalonians' expectation of the imminent return of Christ—or even the belief that the Day of the Lord had, in some sense, already begun (2:2)—had led some of the Thessalonian congregation to stop working. Another factor in their idleness may have been the traditional Greek attitude toward manual labor. In Judaism, labor with one's hands was honorable, to the extent that even rabbis were expected to have a trade.[1] But among Greeks there was a widespread attitude that such work was suitable only for slaves.

Yet another element in the situation may have been a willingness on the part of wealthier members of the congregation to provide for the poor, perhaps particularly at common meals in the course of which the Lord's Supper was observed. Such generosity might have a thoroughly Christian motivation, of course, but in addition, the practice may have been further stimulated by the contemporary patterns in Greek society, in which wealthy patrons provided food and entertainment for gatherings of trade guilds or civic organizations. Some of the Thessalonian Christians may have taken advantage of such generosity.

One more *possible* ingredient may be signaled by the fact that Paul characterizes some of these persons as **busybodies** (3:11). This may be the clue that some of these individuals, freed from work, used their new opportunity to probe into people's lives, supposedly ministering to them, "just wanting to help." They may have thought that this entitled them to be supported by other members of the congregation.

It is obvious that much of this reconstruction is conjectural. But whatever the causes, the problem was real, and Paul insists on its correction. On the other hand, we should not magnify it unduly. If the number involved had been large, Paul would hardly have been as generally commendatory as he is at several points in the letter (for example, 1:3-4; 2:13-14; 3:4). His concern may arise more from the persistence of the problem, in spite of earlier admonitions (1 Thess. 4:11-12; 5:14), than from its magnitude.[2]

Paul's prescription here is a mixture of positive command, personal example, rebuke, and instruction. And it is important to note that he expects the congregation to take responsibility for shaping the lives of their members; they are to participate in the disciplinary process (see comments on 1 Thessalonians 5:14.) So what are they to do?

1. KEEP AWAY 3:6

Once more the address to the Thessalonian Christians is **brothers** (2 Thess. 3:6); Paul is talking *to* members of the family *about* members of the family. But the tone of discourse is military. **Command** (3:6) is the first word in the Greek sentence. Paul means business. And this is not only Paul speaking. He reinforces his own word by invoking **the name of the Lord Jesus Christ,** the highest Authority, designated by His full name. The issue is not merely one of obedience to the founding pastor, but to the divine Lord (1 Thess. 4:8).

The fact that in Christ they are family, then, means that they have an obligation to erring brothers and sisters. Paul is concerned that the local body of Christ should be involved in this disciplinary situation (see 1 Corinthians 5:1-5). Therefore, the first instruction is directed to the obedient majority. The command is to **keep away,** primarily as a form of discipline for the offenders, but perhaps also to keep others from being infected by similar attitudes. Oral warnings when the missionaries were with them, and later written warnings (1 Thess.), have not been enough;

stronger measures are required. Paul calls for the ostracism of the offenders—**keep away**—and the form of the verb implies that this distancing is to be an ongoing process, at least until the discipline has proved effective.

The reason for the treatment is implied by describing the persons involved as **idle** (2 Thess. 3:6). The basic meaning of the word is "disorderly" or, more literally, "out of order." A Greek-English dictionary defines it as "out of order, out of place . . . frequently of soldiers not keeping rank or an army in disarray."[3] The literal Greek in verse 6 describes the person as "walking disorderly," using "walk" to suggest a way of life, thus indicating that these are persons whose lifestyle is at fault. They are habitual, not occasional, offenders. Thus, the New English Bible translates this, "falls into idle habits." Therefore, they are, in the words of A. L. Moore, "in this respect unruly, unwilling to exert themselves, and unwilling to conform to the standard incumbent upon members of the Christian congregation."[4] Later it will be made clear that these people were not merely unemployed; they were *refusing* to work (3:10b).

Does not live according to the teaching you received from us shows that the problem is not one of ignorance. They had received instruction on this point, as part of the common stock of teaching regularly given to converts in the early church (see comments on "tradition" at 2:15). But notice that the offender is still called **brother,** even though he is out of line and under discipline.

2. PAUL'S EXAMPLE 3:7-9

For (2 Thess. 3:7) shows that Paul next moves to justify the action he is calling upon the congregation to take. The loafers are without excuse because they had had Paul's example lived before them. This is significant because it implies that the "tradition," the pattern of teaching for converts, includes the *example* of the missionaries as well as their oral instruction. That example, under God, imposes a duty. The word translated **ought** signals strong moral obligation; it often implies "necessary because it is God's will" and most often is translated "must" (for example, John 3:30; Acts 9:6).

We were not idle is an understatement (see 1 Thessalonians 2:9). Jason was their host in Thessalonica (Acts 17:5), but the missionary team provided their own maintenance, at least for food (2 Thess. 3:8). He reminds the Thessalonian converts of how they **worked night and day, laboring and toiling** (see comments on 1 Thessalonians 2:9).

One reason was **so that we would not be a burden,** but there was more to it than that. Apparently it was Paul's standard policy not to accept support from the people among whom he was planting a church (see 1 Corinthians 9:12, 18; 2 Corinthians 11:7-12; 12:13-18). This (1) gave him independence; (2) safeguarded his freedom in ministry; (3) set a good example; and (4) distinguished him from traveling preachers who made a living by peddling their message (2 Cor. 2:17; 1 Thess. 2:4-9). On occasion, he did accept gifts from a church he had founded *after* he had left them and was laboring elsewhere (see Philippians 4:16). Second Thessalonians 3:9 is a sort of parenthetical remark to explain further Paul's policy and practice (see 1 Corinthians 9 for extended treatment of the apostolic right to financial support; also 2 Corinthians 12:13-18; 1 Timothy 5:18; Matthew 10:9; Luke 10:7-8]).

Paul reiterates (2 Thess. 3:9b; see verse 7) that another purpose for his working among them was **to make ourselves a model for you** (see 1 Thessalonians 1:6-7; 2:14; also 1 Corinthians 4:16; 11:1; Ephesians 5:1; Philippians 3:17; 4:9). As the frequent references show, Paul takes his personal example to be an essential ingredient in his ministry. While acknowledging its difficulty for pastors today, Leon Morris recognizes its importance: "While we feel some diffidence today about appealing to our own example, and while we must recognize that dangers lie there, yet it remains true that no preaching of the gospel can ever be really effective unless the life of the pastor is such as to commend the message."[5]

Paul here probably also intends to make this point: For the sake of the gospel he chose not to make use of his ministerial right to support, and was willing to work for his own maintenance; how much more, then, his readers should expect to provide for themselves as one aspect of their basic Christian duty.

3. PAUL'S COMMAND 3:10

But Paul does not rely on their inferring that lesson just from his example. He gives them the **rule: "If a man will not work, he shall not eat"** (2 Thess. 3:10). The force of the language here would be more clearly expressed by translating, "When we were with you, we used to give you this command;" that is to say, not just once, but repeatedly, as a part of their regular teaching. Evidently this was an element in the "tradition" he passed on (3:6; see 2:15). This means that this policy was not Paul's personal "hang-up," but an aspect of the common apostolic teaching. Leon Morris cites the opinion of a scholar on the life of the early church, Adolf von Harnack: "The new religion did not teach 'the dignity of labour.' What it inculcated was just the *duty* of work."[6]

One other point must be made: The New International Version is perhaps not clear enough that the person in question in 3:10 *declines* to work. Paul is not addressing those involuntarily unemployed, and certainly not those unable to work. In the overall picture, this passage must be kept in balance with other Scriptures setting forth the Christian obligation to provide for those unable to maintain themselves.

4. INSTRUCTION TO THE CONGREGATION 3:11-15

The New International Version omits the "For" in the Greek text at the beginning of 2 Thessalonians 3:11, which indicates that Paul now explains his reason for repeating the instructions he has just reviewed with them. Somehow he has learned that **some,** probably a small minority, have been ignoring his instruction in the first letter, "To mind your own business and to work with your hands . . . so that you will not be dependent on anybody" (1 Thess. 4:11-12). And they are not only non-productive; they are somehow counterproductive. Not only are they **not busy;** they are **busybodies.**

Exactly what was happening is not clear. Ernest Best speculates concerning the nature of their meddling: "Perhaps they were trying to persuade others to discontinue working because of the nearness of Christ's coming, or because manual work is ignoble for free men, children of God, or because they needed more time for personal witnessing."[7]

In any case, with verse 12, Paul turns to address the idlers in strong language. (More recent editions of the New International Version differ from earlier ones in the word order, but they still use the same words, except for omitting "the name." The meaning is not changed, but it is clarified.) **We command and urge,** Paul says, and invokes **the Lord Jesus Christ.** In the strongest terms, he is calling for the lifestyle appropriate for those who acknowledge the lordship of Christ in their lives.

The expression **such people** is not intended to be contemptuous, but does specify the object of his commands. There is no room for playing games; if the shoe fits, put it on. **Settle down** is a bit of a paraphrase; more literally, he is insisting that "working with quietness, they eat their own bread." He echoes his own words from 1 Thessalonians 4:11-12, as he calls for a respectable lifestyle, not only for their own sake, but for the well-being of the whole Christian community. The "with quietness" addresses the **busybodies** and orders them to stop meddling.

With **as for you, brothers** (2 Thess. 3:13), Paul abruptly shifts his address to the faithful majority in the community (in the Greek, **you** is emphasized), and calls upon them to devote themselves to **doing what is right.** This advice could be general (see also Galatians 6:9), but almost certainly is related to the specific situation in view. One aspect of it may be that he is urging them to continue to be generous toward those who need help (1 Thess. 5:14), in spite of the fact that some in the community have been abusing their privileges.

But this does not mean that disciplinary action should not be directed toward those who deserve it—those who persistently defy Paul's **instruction in this letter** (2 Thess. 3:14). The congregation is to **take special note** of such persons. But precisely what this means is unclear. They are to be singled out, identified in some manner, so that the whole congregation will be aware of their identity, because they all share responsibility to participate in the discipline of recalcitrant members (see Matthew 18:17; 1 Timothy 5:20; 1 Corinthians 5:4-5; 2 Corinthians 2:5-11). Paul called upon the congregation to minister to one another in 1 Thessalonians 5:14-15, and this is one aspect of that responsibility.

Apparently these people are to be dealt with individually, as indicated by the singular pronouns **anyone** and **him.** And the specific disciplinary action takes the form of ostracizing: **Do not associate with him.** The word means something like "do not mix yourselves together with him." The same Greek word is used in 1 Corinthians 5:9 (for similar instructions, see Romans 16:17-19; 1 Corinthians 5:9-11; 2 John 10-11). In this case, the purpose of the discipline is remedial: **that he may feel ashamed.** He is to be made aware of his guilt, but not left there. The shame he feels is intended to be a step toward repentance and restoration.

The spirit in which such discipline is administered is crucial: **Do not regard him as an enemy** (2 Thess. 3:15). If the action is perceived by the one disciplined as unfair, partisan, or malicious, the discipline will be counterproductive. Paul advises the Galatians on this point: "Brothers, if someone is caught in a sin, you who are spiritual should restore him gently. But watch yourself, or you also may be tempted" (Gal. 6:1). Obviously, some people will be required to sit in judgment, as it were, and evaluate. The process may be more risky spiritually for them than for the defendant.

Through it all the person is still to be regarded as a **brother** (or sister). With Matthew 18:15 in mind, John Stott comments, "Paul's intention is not that he be excluded from the community, but reinstated in it. Jesus made this plain by saying that if an offender listens to reproof, 'You have won your brother over.'"[8]

Paul did not spell out the judicial procedure, for example who administers it, what steps in the process, who decides when enough is enough, etc. Passages like Matthew 18:15-17; 2 Corinthians 2:5-11; Galatians 6:1-2; 1 Timothy 5:20; and Titus 3:10, suggest that before public discipline was put in motion, there would be private attempts by elders and/or fellow members of the congregation to persuade the offender to acknowledge his fault and mend his ways.

If public censure was required, it is probable that in the Thessalonian situation it took the form of exclusion from the common meal connected with the Lord's Supper. This may be the implication of **he shall not eat** (2 Thess. 3:10). But obviously, such persons were not to be excluded from *all* association; there would have to be some degree of communication if they were to **warn him as a brother.** John Wesley recommended, "Tell him lovingly of the reason why you shun him."[9]

Practical problems in putting these principles into action in the much more complicated contemporary church situation abound, not least that the disciplined person may elect to move to the church down the street. And sadly, he may well be welcomed without any reference to the congregation he has left behind. The saddest aspect is not the loss of a member by the one congregation, but rather that the discipline meant for the member's good failed to secure the intended result in amendment of life and restoration to fellowship.

I. Howard Marshall remarks that direct application of the process Paul outlines is difficult. One reason is "that the nature of the Christian community has changed. Discipline is possible and necessary within a fairly compact, closely-related group, but this may not be so in the rather loose association typical of many modern congregations."[10]

ENDNOTES

[1]Judaism is the life and belief system of the Jewish people and involves a covenant relationship with God. Though there are various branches of Judaism, the underlying theme among them is monotheism and a recognition of the Law, or Torah (the first five books of the Old Testament: Genesis, Exodus, Leviticus, Numbers, and Deuteronomy).

[2]The persistence of the problem may be illustrated by the following recommendations from the *Didache,* an early Christian document usually dated about A.D. 112: "If he who comes is a traveler, help him as much as you can, but he shall not stay with you more than two days, or, if necessary, three. If he wishes to settle down with you and has a craft, let him work for his bread. But if he has no craft, make such provision for him as your intelligence approves, so

that no one shall live with you in idleness as a Christian. If he refuses to do so, he is making merchandise of Christ; beware of such people." Cited in *1 and 2 Thessalonians,* Word Biblical Commentary, by F. F. Bruce (Waco, Texas: Word Books, Publisher,1982), pp. 206–7.

[3]G. Abbott-Smith, *A Manual Greek Lexicon of the New Testament* (Edinburgh: T. and T. Clark, 1937), p. 67.

[4]A. L. Moore, *1 and 2 Thessalonians,* Century Bible (London: Thomas Nelson and Sons, Ltd., 1969), p. 116.

[5]Leon Morris, *The First and Second Epistles to the Thessalonians,* rev. ed., New International Commentary on the New Testament (Grand Rapids, Michigan: Wm. B. Eerdmans Publishing Co., 1991), p. 254.

[6]Ibid., p. 256n.

[7]Ernest Best, *A Commentary on the First and Second Epistles to the Thessalonians,* Harper's New Testament Commentaries (New York: Harper and Row Publishers, 1972), p. 340.

[8]John Stott, *The Gospel and the End of Time* (Downers Grove, Illinois: InterVarsity Press, 1991), p. 194.

[9]John Wesley, *Explanatory Notes upon the New Testament* (London: Epworth Press, 1950), p. 769.

[10]I. Howard Marshall, *1 and 2 Thessalonians,* New Century Bible Commentary (Grand Rapids, Michigan: Wm. B. Eerdmans Publishing Co., 1983), p. 229.

16

CONCLUSION
2 Thessalonians 3:16-18

Paul now brings the letter quickly to a close with a final greeting sandwiched between two sentence prayers.

1. PRAYER FOR PEACE 3:16

We have mentioned that in several letters Paul calls upon "the God of peace" in the closing sections of his letters (for example, 1 Thessalonians 5:23; Romans 15:33; 16:20; 2 Corinthians 13:11; see Philippians 4:7, 9; Colossians 3:15; Galatians 6:16. It is noteworthy that in three of these references, the wish for peace follows words of warning (Rom. 16; 2 Cor. 13; Gal. 6).

It is not obvious why the prayer on this occasion is addressed to **the Lord of peace,** instead of the usual "*God* of peace." This is the only place where the expression is used. The reference almost certainly is to Christ, who is frequently associated with the Father as a source of peace in opening salutations (2 Thess. 1:1; Rom. 1:7b; 1 Cor. 1:3; 2 Cor. 1:2; Gal. 1:3; Phil. 1:2; see Ephesians 1:2). **Peace** was to be the supreme gift of the Messiah (see Isaiah 9:6-7; Micah 5:4-5; Zechariah 9:9-10), and F. F. Bruce notes concerning **the,** "The article before [peace] points to the peace as *his* peace," and Bruce notes the parallel expression in Colossians 3:15.[1]

If his original impulse to pray for their peace is related to the particular problem among the Thessalonians, Paul quickly widens it: **at all times** and **in all ways.** The peace he prays for is continual and unchanging, in spite of circumstances. **In all ways** is, more precisely, "in *every* way," and the Greek word translated "way" is more literally translated *turning*. Christ's peace continually and at every turn in life— this is Paul's prayer. And the added petition, **the Lord be with all of you** brings Christ closer, right into the community. His presence is our peace. And note the inclusive **all,** even those under discipline.

169

2. FINAL GREETING 3:17

Presumably, Paul now takes the pen from the hand of the scribe and finishes the letter in his own handwriting (see Galatians 6:11; Colossians 4:18; 1 Corinthians 16:21)—"With my own hand I write this: Greetings from Paul" (*Good News Bible,* Today's English Version).

The point Paul intends to make in the rest of the sentence is not clear. Many think that he is providing a means of distinguishing genuine letters from forgeries (2 Thess. 2:2); others think he is simply confirming the authenticity and authority of *this* letter without any reference to other letters allegedly from him, as in Colossians 4:18 and Philemon 19. **This is how I write** probably identifies the particular handwriting as his own (Gal. 6:11).

3. BENEDICTION 3:18

The grace of our Lord Jesus Christ be with you all is a standard Pauline benediction, the same as that which concluded 1 Thessalonians (5:28), except for the addition of **all.** We probably should not make too much of the **all** here, since Paul uses it frequently in such contexts. And yet it makes the point that Paul did not intend to exclude anyone at all, not even the idlers, from the blessing of the Lord. Grace, says Charles Erdman, "is for Paul the beginning and the end of the gospel."[2]

ENDNOTES

[1]F. F. Bruce, *1 and 2 Thessalonians,* Word Biblical Commentary (Waco, Texas: Word Books, Publisher, 1982), p. 212.

[2]Charles Erdman, *The Epistles of Paul to the Thessalonians* (Philadelphia: The Westminster Press, 1935), p. 101.

SELECT BIBLIOGRAPHY

Abbott-Smith, G. *A Manual Greek Lexicon of the New Testament.* Edinburgh: T. and T. Clark, 1937.

Arndt, William F. and F. Wilbur Gingrich. *A Greek-English Lexicon of the New Testament and Other Early Christian Literature.* Chicago, Illinois: The University of Chicago Press, 1957.

Barclay, William. *A New Testament Wordbook.* New York: Harper and Brothers, Publishers, n.d.

Berkhof, Louis. *Systematic Theology.* Grand Rapids, Michigan: Wm. B. Eerdmans Publishing Co., 1941.

Best, Ernest. *A Commentary on the First and Second Epistles to the Thessalonians,* Harper's New Testament Commentaries. New York: Harper and Row Publishers, 1972.

Bewley, Marius. *The Selected Poetry of John Donne.* New York: New American Library, 1966.

Bruce, F. F. *1 and 2 Thessalonians*, Word Biblical Commentary. Waco, Texas: Word Books, Publisher, 1982.

Denney, James. *The Epistles to the Thessalonians,* Expositor's Bible. New York: George H. Doran Co., n.d.

Denney, James. *The Death of Christ.* New York: George H. Doran Co., n.d.

Elias, Jacob W. *1 and 2 Thessalonians,* Believer's Church Bible Commentary. Scottdale, Pennsylvania: Herald Press, 1995.

Ellicott, C. J., ed. *Bible Commentary: The New Testament,* vol. 9, Cambridge Bible for Schools and Colleges. London: Cassell and Co., Ltd., 1887.

Erdman, Charles. *The Epistles of Paul to the Thessalonians.* Philadelphia: The Westminster Press, 1935.

Findlay, George G. *The Epistles to the Thessalonians,* Cambridge Bible for Schools and Colleges. Cambridge: Cambridge University Press, 1894.

Guthrie, D. and J. A. Motyer, eds. *The New Bible Commentary,* rev. ed. Grand Rapids, Michigan: Wm. B. Eerdmans Publishing Co., 1970.

Hawthorne, Gerald F. and Ralph P. Martin, eds. *Dictionary of Paul and His Letters.* Downers Grove, Illinois: InterVarsity Press, 1993.

Hiebert, D. E. *The Thessalonian Letters.* Chicago: Moody Press, 1971.

Hock, Ronald F. *The Social Context of Paul's Ministry: Tentmaking and Apostleship.* Philadelphia: Fortress Press, 1980.

Keck, Leander E. and Victor Paul Furnish. *The Pauline Letters.* Nashville: Abingdon Press, 1984.

Marshall, I. Howard. *1 and 2 Thessalonians,* New Century Bible Commentary. Grand Rapids, Michigan: Wm. B. Eerdmans Publishing Co., 1983.

Milligan, George. *St. Paul's Epistles to the Thessalonians.* Grand Rapids, Michigan: Wm. B. Eerdmans Publishing Co., 1952.

Moore, A. L. *1 and 2 Thessalonians,* Century Bible. London: Thomas Nelson and Sons, Ltd., 1969.

Morris, Leon. *The Epistles of Paul to the Thessalonians,* Tyndale New Testament Commentary. Grand Rapids, Michigan: Wm. B. Eerdmans Publishing Co., 1957.

Morris, Leon. *The First and Second Epistles to the Thessalonians,* rev. ed., New International Commentary on the New Testament. Grand Rapids, Michigan: Wm. B. Eerdmans Publishing Co., 1991.

Plummer, Alfred. *The General Epistles of St. James and St. Jude,* Expositor's Bible. London: Hodder and Stoughton, 1891.

Ries, Claude A. "A Greek New Testament Approach to the Teaching of the Deeper Spiritual Life." Ph.D. diss., Northern Baptist Theological Seminary, 1945.

Stott, John. *The Gospel and the End of Time.* Downers Grove, Illinois: InterVarsity Press, 1991.

Wanamaker, Charles A. *The Epistles to the Thessalonians,* New International Greek Testament Commentary. Grand Rapids, Michigan: Wm. B. Eerdmans Publishing Co., 1990.

Ward, Ronald. *Commentary on 1 and 2 Thessalonians.* Waco, Texas: Word Books, Publisher, 1973.

Wesley, John. *Explanatory Notes upon the New Testament.* London: Epworth Press, 1950.

Wesley, John. *A Plain Account of Christian Perfection.* London: Epworth Press, 1952.

Wesley, John. *The Works of John Wesley*, vol. 14. Grand Rapids, Michigan: Zondervan Publishing House, n.d.

Williams, David. *1 and 2 Thessalonians*, New International Bible Commentary. Peabody, Massachusetts: Hendrickson Publishers, 1992.